Careers and
Opportunities in | **JOURNALISM**

JOURNALISTS AT WORK: 100 to 200 Washington correspondents from every news media attend President's press conference. (*AP Photo*)

Careers and
Opportunities in

JOURNALISM

BY IRA HENRY FREEMAN
AND BEATRICE O. FREEMAN

New York: *E. P. Dutton & Company, Inc.*   1966

Published simultaneously in Canada by Clarke, Irwin & Company
Limited, Toronto and Vancouver

Library of Congress Catalog Card Number: 66-11553

Contents

Illustrations

Foreword |

When our astronauts blast off, when our soldiers go into battle, when revolution explodes, when a President is inaugurated— whenever anything of moment happens anywhere—you are there with notebook, camera, or tape recorder to tell the world all about it.

You are a journalist. You jet about the earth recording history as it is made, interviewing the great, the glamorous, the greatly infamous.

A wild dream of romantic youth? Not necessarily. Such opportunity is there to be seized. There are some reporters who always seem to be where the action is. But that is not the whole story of journalism by a long stick of type.

Many a reporter spends his life in a small town (or a big town, for that matter), never covering a war or interviewing the President. Many an editor is chained to his desk. Many a newsman never sees his by-line in print, or appears on the TV screen, or is heard on the air. Nevertheless, they too lead interesting lives and do important work—more important in our complex, modern world than ever before.

To make up your mind whether to become a journalist, you need the whole picture: what journalists do in every medium of mass communications—newspapers, broadcasting, magazines, public relations; what their satisfactions and dissatisfactions are, what they need to achieve success, what their pay is to start and later, how to get a job and how to prepare for it.

This book purposes to give the facts on which you can make a decision.

Although the authors have spent thirty years in journalism, writing a book of this scope would have been impossible without the aid of hundreds of editors, teachers, and other authorities. To all those who generously contributed their knowledge and advice and who are quoted in the book, we express gratitude.

We are no less grateful to the many others who also provided valuable material but who are not mentioned in the text. For such help we now thank Ruth Adler of *The New York Times*, Ellis Baker and Dale E. Larson of the American Newspaper Guild, John E. Stempel of the American Council on Education for Journalism, Robert Chandler of CBS, Joseph Derby of NBC, William Giglio of the American Business Press, Mrs. Donna J. Pierre of the Public Relations Society of America, L. R. Baker of the United States Information Service, Mrs. Dorothy Laves Wolchansky of Theta Sigma Phi, and Ted Boyle of The Associated Press.

1

IS JOURNALISM FOR YOU?

Chapter One
THE PROFESSION
HAS CHANGED

A newspaper correspondent trekked deep into the African bush not long ago. No famine, revolt, or tribal war had occurred. In fact, nothing unusual was happening. Yet, for two weeks he lived in a native settlement, observing, asking questions through an interpreter. His assignment? To bring back an account of day-to-day life in a remote Congolese village.

Journalists take endless pains these days to bring back information beyond traditional "news."

If you become a newsman now—whether for a newspaper, magazine, or broadcasting company—you will surely be occupied with more than an old-fashioned chronicle of daily happenings: public events, acts of government and industry, battles, crimes, accidents, deaths, births, the weather.

Not that this "spot," or "hard," news is neglected. On the contrary, we get more of it from all over the earth than ever before. But newsmen augment it now by descriptions of how people live and work, sketches of personalities in the news, investigations of social problems, interpretations of political and economic situations, explanations of scientific discoveries.

REPORTING-IN-DEPTH

Your interests as a journalist will not only be more extensive, they will be "deeper." "Reporting-in-depth" is the hallmark of modern journalism.

A suburban newspaper on Long Island recently assigned a staff reporter to investigate the problem of local teen-age drug addiction. His resulting report-in-depth ran to eight installments of four columns each.

The New York Times, a pioneer in this technique, gave reporter Robert Doty a full month to produce his eight-column study of male homosexuality.

Even magazines like *The New Yorker,* founded as a weekly of sophisticated humor, depend heavily on in-depth reporting. *The New Yorker,* in fact, led the way with John Hersey's study of Hiroshima after the atom bomb fell. Hersey worked for a year on the report, and the magazine devoted virtually an entire issue to it.

In its "specials," television, newest medium of journalism, probes contemporary problems as varied as urban blight, abuse of children, the hard life of Andean tin miners. NBC gave a large staff five months to prepare a three-hour "White Paper" on United States foreign policy.

In all media, a new dimension has been added to the reporting of spot news, too.

Few newsmen any longer limit their reports to the classic four Ws: *Who* did *What, When,* and *Where.* A fifth W, *Why,* has been added; it is as important as any of the others and treated more extensively.

There is argument today as to whether, despite these developments, the quality of American journalism has been improving. Some critics contend there has been a decline. They point to the disappearance of more than a few intellectual quarterly and monthly magazines and some daily newspapers that used to circulate among a cultural elite. But they overlook the fact that the popular and average level of all newspapers, magazines, and broadcast journalism is higher than ever.

The improvement was inevitable to keep pace with the rising educational standard of the American people. As that standard keeps rising, journalistic standards will go on rising, too.

THE CHANGED NEWSMAN

Better journalism requires better journalists; intelligent, educated men with a serious attitude toward their work.

You may have seen old movies portraying the newsman as a police reporter—tough, shrewd, cynical, immature, with a bottle of gin in his pocket and a hole in his shoe. There were some newspapermen like them once, but the breed is extinct now.

Judith Crist, an experienced reporter, and movie critic of the *New York Herald Tribune*, celebrated the change on the twenty-fifth anniversary of the American Newspaper Guild with an article in *The Columbia University Forum:*

> Step into my city room. . . . Here you will find no one rushing about shouting, "Stop the presses!" or "Hold Page One for a hot exclusive!" The managing editor does not stand glued to a telephone listening to a legman. . . . There are no crap games going on in corners, no fedora-topped drunkards tippling from desk drawer bottles, no wily reporters solving crimes with evidence they have stolen from the scene, no practical jokers reveling in writing fake stories. . . .
>
> I look about me at the clean-shirted, barbered, shaven and sober commuters who are my colleagues. . . . The postwar newspaperman has come into his own at last as a professional.

Miss Christ sees no loss of glamor in the change.

> Sane, sober and secure though this business has become, it has lost none of the glory that is its essence—of transmitting the fact, of telling the truth so that people will know it, and, one must confess, of being on the inside when news is made.
>
> None of the fun has gone out either. If anything, the company is better, the wit more sophisticated, joking less juvenile, iconoclasm more judicious and the occasional bender all the better for its occasion. And something has been added, a sense of service beyond oneself and a consciousness of craft: in short, professional pride.

Chapter Two | **WHAT JOURNALISM OFFERS**

Journalism is not a "game", as outsiders sometimes call it. It is true that a few columnists manage to play it that way, that to every newsman some free champagne and caviar must fall, that some assignments are so much fun it seems a shame to take your pay. Nevertheless, however much the work may be enjoyed, it has a serious, social purpose.

That purpose is to give news and all the accessory information and guidance the people need to run society.

We in America today are so stuffed with news that we take it for granted. But try to imagine how we would live if news were suddenly shut off, if we never read a newspaper and never heard a news broadcast. We could not sustain civilization.

The press is essential to *any* modern society, but a *free* press is vital to democracy. Our Founding Fathers recognized that when they guaranteed a free press in Article I of the "Bill of Rights."

"Were it left to me to decide whether we should have a government without newspapers or newspapers without a government, I should not hesitate a moment to choose the latter," said Thomas Jefferson, author of the "Bill of Rights."

It is significant that to this day no dictatorship, right or left, has been able to tolerate a free press.

THE CHANCE TO SERVE

Using its freedom, the press in our country has been the most powerful weapon guarding the people's liberties, righting wrongs, combating evil.

For such public service, Pulitzer Prizes have been awarded to journalists annually since 1917. The citations are inspiring stories of exposing corruption, vindicating innocent men, defending civil rights. The honor roll includes editors of tiny weeklies as well as correspondents of great dailies, legmen as well as publishers.

It takes exceptional ability and employer support to win a public service Pulitzer award. You may never make it, but you can brighten the corner where you work. Your hard-hitting story from Washington or the state capital may correct a bad government policy; your feature on a cancer campaign may save a life; your review may bring recognition to an unknown talent; you may influence farmers to raise needed sugar beets instead of surplus cotton; you may inspire a bright youth to become a scientist like one you have interviewed; your exposé of dirty restaurant kitchens may force strict health inspections.

Whether you bring your community news of the local school board, or the entire country news of the United Nations, as a journalist you always perform a public service, though in varying degree.

VARIETY

Some temperaments thrive on never knowing what the day will bring. If you are that way, newswork will attract you. Like Cleopatra, news is of infinite variety.

Scan any metropolitan newspaper: more than a hundred stories of things that occurred that day on earth—and beyond—from war in Vietnam to a new teen-age country club, from the new Paris fashions to firing of a moon rocket. The editors had to put their minds on every story; each copyreader on eight to twenty; each rewrite man on half a dozen; each reporter perhaps on only one, but it was different from the story he did yesterday and from the one he will do tomorrow.

A similar variety spices work on broadcast news and on news magazines.

Variety is not diminished as you go down the scale to less

important vehicles of news. Quite the reverse. One of the compensations of working for a country weekly, for instance, is that you will do many more different jobs than you will ever get a chance at on a big daily. And the one newsman for a small radio station will do everything in microcosm which the huge staff of CBS News does.

SUCH INTERESTING PEOPLE

You may have heard the bromide, "the nice thing about journalism is you meet so many interesting people." Well, it is quite true. Uninteresting people don't get written up, or if they do, it is by doing something remarkable for once in their dull lives.

Naturally, it is the reporter who has the best chance to meet interesting people.

And most of the interesting people—the makers and shakers of the world, heads of states, leaders of art and thought, glamor queens, the famous cooks—are to be found in the greatest centers. That is what makes New York such an exciting place for a reporter to work.

Yet even the reporter in a small town will meet the most interesting people in that town. In the course of his work, he will get to know the residents of importance and interview the visiting firemen.

As for those offbeat, colorful characters who are not important personages but excellent feature copy, they abound everywhere.

The press has such a privileged position in America that it is easy for a reporter to get an interview with almost anyone. Usually all he need do is call upon the news source and introduce himself. Even if he spots a news source on the street, anyone from gangster to archbishop, the reporter is suffered to walk right up and ask questions.

Nor is he restricted to polite questions. However august the interviewee, the reporter goes right to the heart of the matter with direct questions, no matter how personal or even embarrassing.

Going after news, reporters have asked questions for which non-journalists would be thrown out. They have questioned the

President about his private income, heads of states about secret treaties, actresses about their sex affairs, a queen about her children's misbehavior, a distinguished author about the failure of his book. The interviewee does not have to answer, but he cannot stop the questions.

It is becoming common practice for editors also to go out on an occasional story for a first-hand impression that will help them in editing. In addition, editors are sometimes taken into private conferences by high government and corporation officers, meetings from which reporters are barred. One of the fascinations of journalism is being "in on the know," getting the "inside stuff," even if you cannot print it for the time being.

SUCCESS ON MERIT

One of the solid satisfactions in journalism is that success depends largely upon merit, at least in the great majority of jobs among writers and working editors.

Writing or editing a story is like playing the violin; you do it all by yourself, well or badly, according to your ability; you cannot fake it; no one can do it for you. Nor do connections help you. Though nepotism may get you a job, it cannot produce a story.

There are judges whose learned opinions are written by bright law clerks, and architects whose beautiful plans are drawn by obscure employes, but the story under a reporter's by-line is done by himself. He may have been aided by legmen and a copyreader, but in most cases that aid was secondary.

CREATIVE SATISFACTION

Writing is not only a means of communication but also, inevitably, of self-expression. It is natural to take satisfaction in it; if you did not, you would not want to become a journalist.

Jimmy Breslin, the *New York Herald Tribune*'s syndicated columnist, has put it this way:

The hours are strange and they make life strange, too, but always there is one big thing going for you. Write a story

and in a matter of hours you can walk through a subway
train and spot somebody with his eyes on your story and
there is a feeling that the kind of life you're leading is
worthwhile. Oh, you're not doing some big thing. You're
just putting out something that a person can get some information from, maybe even enjoy. In a couple of seconds,
the feeling is gone. . . . But a lot of people go through their
whole lives and never know what it is to get satisfaction
out of a job.

The kick is doubled if the story carries your by-line or your
face appears on the screen. No matter what success you may
ultimately achieve, no triumph will give you the delicious jolt
of that first by-line as a cub, even if it was on the last page of a
country weekly.

While a by-line serves the utilitarian purpose of building a
writer's reputation and thereby his earning potential, it also feeds
his ego. And we are all weak enough to enjoy that.

Some veterans never get over being "by-line happy." They
keep their names in the paper even on vacations, will not permit
substitutes to write their columns, refuse executive positions
because they entail anonymity. Some writers have declined to
work on *Time* magazine, only because there are no by-lines.

Journalism is one of the quickest routes to celebrity of a kind.
Do one good story and the next day praise pours in by mail and
telephone. When you go out on your next assignment you are
treated with new respect. Magazine and book editors solicit you
to write for them. Fame can come literally overnight.

PERQUISITES

The American journalist enjoys certain perequisites that are
minor but pleasant. Since the press is the most powerful molder
of public opinion, everyone who depends upon publicity cul-
tivates the goodwill of reporters and editors. Though the wise
journalist realizes he is loved for his paper and not for himself,
it is nice to be wooed. When he covers a dinner, he is dined and
wined at a press table. Press agents and government officials are

glad to do him a personal favor. Without having to wait in the outer office, he is shown promptly into the presence of the Great Man. He is passed through police barriers, behind the scenes at the opera, into Congressional press galleries. He rides behind the hero at a parade, in the governor's private plane. The mayor calls him by his first name.

Some profess to disdain these things as trivial, as conferring a false status. Nevertheless, everyone wants status, and journalists enjoy more status, deserved or not, than many business and professional men of higher income.

CAMARADERIE

Finally, there is a camaraderie among journalists that is attractive. Rival reporters often pool their information on big, diffuse stories. Among newspapermen it is traditional to file a story for a colleague who has been physically prevented from doing it himself.

You will not find many phonies or stuffed shirts among newsmen. They are typically free-thinking, iconoclastic fellows, lacking in reverence, no respectors of rank or dignity, including their own. They cover up any sentimentality or idealism by a pretense of cynicism. They are clannish; among themselves, they are witty, ribald, and never tire of talking shop.

Chapter Three | DISADVANTAGES TO CONSIDER

Now, before you dash off to offer your body, soul, and portable typewriter to the nearest editor, consider there are disadvantages in journalism, as in other careers.

Excitement, yes; but there are not enough exciting assignments to go around the staff every day. For every correspondent traipsing around exotic places, dozens of deskbound Joes and Janes are rewriting handouts and editing routine news in the home office. As a beginner, the dullest assignments will go to you; and later on, depend upon it, you will fail to get all the good assignments you think you deserve.

That public service you burn to perform! How vital is covering a P.T.A. luncheon, a holdup of a liquor store, a bank president's fiftieth anniversary? Any reporter has his share of trivial stories; a young reporter, a very large share.

Besides, not every newspaper, radio or television station, or magazine has the crusading spirit to make war on rascals in high places. And without an outlet, even a Lincoln Steffens is powerless to effect reform.

WRITERS' CRAMPS

Inevitably there are writers' frustrations. The story on which you labored so hard may be killed by the editor for another more important. Copyreaders may edit out your vivid description, your singing metaphor. In the composing room, makeup men may drop your punch line for space. It happens to the best of writers.

In the novel *Erik Dorn,* the city editor walking home at dawn sees his discarded newspaper lining garbage cans and blowing along the gutter. That's what happens to most of the work of journalists. "Nothing is so dead as yesterday's newspaper."

Well, a journalist must not allow himself to weep over that. For him, "every morn is the world made new." However, there is a warning to be given here to students of purely literary ambition.

When journalism students are polled as to why they chose that calling, all of them reply, "because I want to write"; half of them cite this as their most compelling reason. If by saying, "I want to write," you mean poetry, fiction, or belles lettres, you will not satisfy the need to express yourself by turning out news and feature articles. The editor who admires your short stories or verse does not wish to encourage you in that direction, but to turn your talent to his purpose.

And his purpose, journalistic writing, is not only different from literature, but antagonistic to it. Journalism will give you speed and facility in writing, but it may also destroy your individuality and vulgarize your style.

In *The Summing Up,* Somerset Maugham asserted:

People who write much for the press seem to lose the faculty of seeing things for themselves; they see them from a generalized standpoint, vividly often, sometimes with hectic brightness, yet never with that idiosyncrasy which may give only a partial picture but is suffused by the personality of the observer. The press kills the individuality of those who write for it.

Cyril Connolly, the British critic, adds:

A writer who takes up journalism abandons the slow tempo of literature for a faster one, and the change will do him harm. The flippancy of journalism will become a habit, and the pleasure of being paid on the nail, and of being praised on the nail, grow indispensable.

There have been some journalists, like Allen Drury and John Hersey, who later became successful novelists, but they are few. There also have been some creative authors who were once journalists, like Ernest Hemingway and Carl Sandburg, but only briefly.

If you want to write, it is best to make up your mind whether it is to be journalism or art, and concentrate on one or the other.

HOME LIFE?

A normal social life—surely everyone has a right to that? Not a journalist!

When Margaret Truman, daughter of former President Harry S Truman, married *The New York Times* correspondent E. Clifton Daniel, his colleague, James B. Reston, gave her a piece of wry advice:

It's not a reporter's working hours that count, but the hours he works. These are regulated by the news, and the news is regulated by a very simple, mathematical rule. This is, that the news of the day, no matter how trivial or unimportant, always takes up more time than a married man has.

For many a journalist, a normal social or home life is impossible. Since news occurs around the clock 365 days a year, somebody must work the night shifts, on week ends, on Christmas and New Year's. As a beginner that probably means you!

If your story is still running when quitting time arrives, you stick with it even if it goes on all night.

Since news has an inconsiderate way of breaking without warning, you may be sent out of town without advance notice. We know a top correspondent who was dispatched to remote Iran on the very day his only son was stricken with polio.

An out-of-town assignment you expect to last one day may

go on for six weeks. The job of roving reporter will keep you away from home 80 percent of the time. You may get an offer of a foreign post—but in Léopoldville or Saigon, where you cannot take your wife and children.

If you insist upon a secure home life as well as a journalistic career, your best bet would be a desk job, like rewrite or editing, on a monthly magazine or company house organ. The hours are conventional and the pressure much less than on a daily newspaper, a wire service, or in news broadcasting.

Some journalists seek to solve the problem by marrying other journalists. Not infrequently, such couples compound their difficulties because their hours cannot be synchronized. But, at least, there are no quarrels on that score!

WOMEN'S PROBLEMS

The problem of combining a professional career with homemaking is especially difficult for women journalists. It is a wonder that so many have succeeded.

There are husband-and-wife teams of foreign correspondents whose children have gone to school in four countries and in as many languages, without harm. There are quite a number of energetic women reporters, copyreaders, and editors who manage to run a house, care for a husband and raise two or three children, despite out-of-town assignments and working nights.

Long maternity leaves, which have become standard in journalism, help. Some women resign to raise a family, then return after their children are grown.

"That's one of the advantages of journalism for a woman," says Mrs. Elizabeth Bernkopf, who began a second career on the *Boston Globe* at the age of fifty-five. "It's a craft you are not likely to forget. And since you read newspapers and magazines and listen to radio and watch television anyway, you automatically keep up with changes and new trends."

Other women have made the best of two worlds by writing magazine or newspaper supplement features at home, or by doing occasional publicity work, or by acting as "stringer" correspondents in their local community for metropolitan newspapers.

STRAIN AND DANGER

Journalism is not to be classed with perilous occupations like test-piloting, for instance. Yet, it often inflicts nervous tension, phyiscal strain, sometimes danger to life.

Since World War II, it has become routine for bold young war correspondents to leave the official communiqués and the "big picture" to their offices in the rear, while they go under fire to bring back vignettes of the actual fighting.

In World War II, forty-five American journalists were killed and 122 wounded in battle or injured in airplane and jeep crashes. Larry Allen of the A.P. made some kind of record by being shelled, shot at with rifles and machine guns, bombed, torpedoed, and half-drowned.

Since then, in Korea, Vietnam, the Congo, in every Latin American revolution, the newsman has been "pursuing the bubble, reputation, even in the cannon's mouth." Five correspondents were killed in Vietnam in one year, three in one forty-day period. In recent conflicts we have seen television correspondents broadcasting from fighting zones and heard their voices against the rattle of machine guns and the boom of mortar fire.

What reporting under fire is like was described by Malcolm Browne, co-winner of a Pulitzer Prize for international reporting, to members of the Overseas Press Club:

"We work a seven-day week in Saigon. . . . Violent news sometimes happens a grenade's throw from the office. During the coup last November 1, we had some close shaves. The fighting began early in the afternoon. . . . We split up . . . leaving Ed White . . . on the desk in the office.

"We called in or came in periodically, sometimes ducking through holes in the walls to get out of the path of strafing fighters. By nightfall, the fighting was close to the palace—and the office. . . . None of us could get in or reach Ed by phone.

"Finally at 7:00 P.M., Ed . . . made it out to the defense perimeter. A few hours later, two palace guards were killed on the balcony over the office and their blood covered the front of the building. . . . A tank blew up twenty feet from the office door."

SOUND OF FIRING, VOICE OVER: TV correspondent broadcasts account of battle in Vietnam. (*CBS*)

War correspondents are not the only journalists exposed to danger of death. Don Mellett of the *Canton* (Ohio) *Daily News* was shot dead by gangsters for his exposure of underworld operations in his city. George Polk disappeared while investigating a revolutionary situation in Greece and was never seen or heard of again. Will Barber of the *Chicago Tribune* caught malaria in the Ethiopian desert and dictated his last story from a hospital bed just before he died.

"The physical danger and strain of covering news increased

abroad and at home," Wes Gallagher, general manager of The Associated Press, said in his annual report for 1964. He cited not only the fighting in Vietnam and the Congo, but also racial rioting in the United States and the jet campaigning of the national election, which "made political reporting a contest of endurance."

Not all journalistic jobs are that hard or dangerous. But the most exciting assignments tend to be. If you refuse to undertake any strain or risk, you probably won't go very far in journalism. There is unavoidable tension of the deadline in most jobs, at the very least; journalists suffer their share of occupational stomach ulcers and heart attacks.

Chapter Four

THE OPPORTUNITIES
AND PAY

As for finding a job in journalism, the good word is, don't worry
about it. The job will come looking for you. At this moment and
for the foreseeable future, there is a job in journalism for every
qualified young college graduate—not a job on *The New York
Times, Life* magazine, or CBS, but a job at a reasonable wage on
a good newspaper or magazine, radio or television station.

Indeed, there is an overabundance of jobs.

"The mass communications industry today is facing a serious
logistics problem; the demand for qualified young people to fill
important jobs in the industry far exceeds the supply," says Richard W. Budd, assistant director of the University of Iowa School
of Journalism.

"By conservative estimate, at least 5,000 new journalists a year
are required to fill existing opportunities," says Paul S. Swensson,
executive director of The Newspaper Fund. "A nationwide survey, if one were made, might double that number.

"The decade of the seventies promises even more opportunities
in journalism. The visible supply of talented young people falls
far short of the demand."

It is true that the number of English language dailies in the
United States was only 1,754 in 1964—311 morning papers and
1,453 evening papers, including 10 with both morning and afternoon editions, much below the peak of 2,600 dailies in 1910.

Publishers insist, however, that their industry is flourishing.
They point out that the decline in number of papers has virtually

stopped for the last five years, while total circulation has risen to over sixty million and advertising volume and revenue continually forge to new highs. Newspapers still give jobs to slightly more than half of all employed journalists in the country; total newspaper employment has gone up 31 percent since the end of World War II as contrasted with only 9 percent in manufacturing. About 10 percent of the total editorial force must be replaced each year, and while mechanical and clerical employes of newspapers are threatened with automation, journalists are not.

There is no computer yet invented to cover a story, write it, edit it, or think up assignments. The old-fashioned human brain still serves the newsman better than anything else.

Predictions are that other segments of journalism—particularly business and industrial publications and broadcast news—will go on expanding.

It is no wonder that employers vie for the cream of each year's crop. College placement bureaus are deluged with requests for promising seniors, even juniors, or graduates one or two years out of school. There are active campus recruitment campaigns, particularly by newspapers.

"All our graduates will get jobs at the end of the school year, except the few boys who go into military service or the Peace Corps or the girls who become housewives," says Professor Richard Baker, associate dean of Columbia University, Graduate School of Journalism.

"Every spring, editors descend upon us to interview applicants, and upon all the other leading journalism schools as well. Some papers and magazines have regular recruiters who tour the country looking for talent. Each of them has openings for four to a dozen youngsters each spring. They come from all over the country; they don't like to pick all their staff from their local area, for some reason. And there are frequent calls upon us during the school year for talented youngsters."

However, most of the top teams in the big leagues do no recruiting. Some do take a few "internes" or trainees on a summer tryout basis. Most do not, and there are seldom any openings on their staffs for absolute beginners. Even positions as copyboys are fought over, and by holders of master's degrees too.

Nevertheless, it is surprising how many publications and electronic stations just below the top rank are actively recruiting. Placement directors of journalism schools say there is a choice among four or five jobs open to every graduate. These jobs are not to be disdained. They give valuable experience to qualify you in four or five years for the big teams. The great majority of staffmen on the biggest papers, magazines, and electronic stations started their careers on small units. In fact such experience is usually a prerequisite of employment on the great staffs.

JOBS FOR WOMEN

Opportunities for women in journalism are more limited than for men. A nationwide survey of employment of beginners showed men outnumbering women two to one on daily newspapers, more than that in radio and television, and three to one in wire services.

However, discrimination is decreasing all the time. Women now outnumber men as beginners on weekly papers, on magazines, in public relations, and two to one in teaching of journalism.

The best opportunities for women, according to Professor Gretchen Kemp of Indiana University, head of the Theta Sigma Phi "talent sparks" program, are in women's news on big dailies, general reporting on small and suburban papers, employe publications, and teaching journalism in high schools.

CHANCES FOR NEGROES

In the last few years, there has been a determined rush by employers in journalism, as in other industries outside the South, to prove their hiring practices are not discriminatory.

"Today, many newspapers have one or more Negroes on their staffs," the American Newspaper Guild reports. "In a number of big cities—New York, Detroit, Philadelphia, Toledo and St. Louis, for example—employment has expanded rapidly. One St. Louis paper added eight Negroes in various editorial jobs in the space of one year. In San Francisco and Oakland, Negroes have been hired for the first time—three as reporters, and one as a photographer."

Negroes have recently been added for outside, as well as inside, jobs on radio and television news, and they appear on camera, too.

On the whole, Negroes say they have not had a bad reception.

"I never found being a Negro a disadvantage in working for a daily," says Ted Poston, veteran reporter for the *New York Post*. "On the contrary, it was often an advantage."

"On rare occasions, we heard someone say he was surprised to find a Negro reporter covering a white function, but if there has been a complaint, I have not heard of it," says Joseph Paull, assisting managing editor of the *Washington Post*.

Managing editors say they cannot find enough qualified Negroes, but Negro leaders retort that editors demand higher qualifications of Negroes than of whites.

"They expect every Negro boy to be a Ted Poston, a Dale Wright, a Carl Rowan, or a George Brown," they say. "These are exceptional reporters regardless of color, winners of national awards, high government press officers. Editors don't demand that of every white cub."

EARNINGS

Average earnings of journalists are often compared unfavorably with those of physicians, lawyers, dentists, engineers, and scientists in private industry. This comparison is not entirely valid, because those learned professions require more education and quite different talents from those needed in journalism.

The pay of journalists surpasses that of some other professional wage-employes—such as schoolteachers, social workers, civil service workers—which require about the same amount of education.

The Newspaper Fund has been collecting statistics on starting wages for all graduates of journalism schools annually since 1960.

The national averages for 1965, as given by Patrick W. Kennedy, assistant to the director of the Fund, were: weekly newspapers, $92.17; wire services, $101.78; radio, $100.38; daily newspapers, $95.74; television, $90.67; public relations, $105.63; magazines (including house organs) $104.14. The average has been rising by 5 percent a year, but is still too low to attract enough good people to fill all the vacancies.

Mr. Kennedy notes, however, that more than 40 percent of the beginning salaries were above average, ranging up to $8,320 a year. Graduates of graduate schools, and the top graduates of leading undergraduate schools, commanded better-than-average starting wages.

It is general practice for employers to grant rapid and frequent pay rises to hold young journalists in the first three to six years. In fact, minimum increases are required in many organizations by union contract. Practically every competent newsman will make a living wage after about five years.

It is after that that dissatisfaction with pay sets in. Many journalists feel they are stuck on a kind of plateau that rises only with the cost of living. Big wages to working journalists (excluding top executives) in the media go only to top men on the few biggest papers, national magazines, and syndicates, and three major radio-television networks. Some top newspapermen and magazine writers earn $50,000 a year, television "anchormen" $100,000 to $200,000. But, perhaps only 5 percent of journalists earn above $25,000 a year.

It is not surprising, therefore, that the late Professor George J. Kienzle, director of Ohio State University School of Journalism, found in a recent survey that 70 percent of journalists quit the mass media within ten years after college.

"Ten years after graduation only three out of ten graduates are in media (newspapers, news broadcasting, news and general magazines)," he reported, "and only two of those three are certain they intend to stay. Only one of every six graduates is in the newspaper newsroom.

"The economics are obvious: seven out of ten who left quit because the pay was too low. Others changed jobs for reasons tied to the pay scale, or to personnel policies and operating practices that would cost money to change. Those who left for a bigger future saw also a bigger pay check in that future."

Half of those who left went into public relations, one-third into house organs and subsidized trade papers, and one-tenth into other business. Doubling, even tripling their pay was not uncommon.

If money is very important to you, your best chance is in the semi-journalistic fields of public relations and promotional publications.

FOR MORE INFORMATION

BOOKLETS, PAMPHLETS

Balk, Al. *The Big Story.* Sigma Delta Chi, 35 East Wacker Dr., Chicago, Ill. 60601. Free

Choosing a Career in Journalism. American Council on Education for Journalism, Ernie Pyle Hall, University of Indiana, Bloomington, Ind. 35¢

Journalism as a Career. #19, Careers Research Monographs, Institute for Research, 537 South Dearborn, Chicago 5, Ill. $1

Journalist. B-8R, Career Briefs. Careers, Largo, Fla. 25¢

One Hundred Books for New Journalists. Bibliography. The Newspaper Fund, P.O. Box 300, Princeton, N.J. Free.

PERIODICALS

Columbia Journalism Review. Quarterly. Columbia University, New York, N.Y.

Iowa Publisher. Monthly. Iowa University School of Journalism, Iowa City, Iowa. Special issue, *Career Opportunities in Journalism.* 50¢

Nieman Reports. Irregularly. Nieman Alumni Council, 44 Holyoke House, Cambridge 38, Mass.

The Matrix. Bimonthly, Theta Sigma Phi, journalism sorority. P.O. Box 7619, University Station, Austin, Texas.

The Quill. Monthly, Sigma Delta Chi, journalism society, 35 East Wacker Dr., Chicago, Ill. $5 a year. Special issue, *Journalism Careers, Opportunities.* 30¢

SPECIAL HELP FOR NEGROES

Human Rights Department, American Newspaper Guild. 1126 16th St., N.W., Washington, D.C.

Skills Bank, National Urban League. 14 East 48th St., New York, N.Y.

Chapter Five | WHAT IT TAKES

Standards of writing throughout journalism are higher than ever before. Brilliant writers will find more opportunities and higher pay, not only on magazine and television staffs, but also on newspapers.

All editors welcome writing talent; some insist upon it as a primary requisite.

"More than anything else I want to see superior writing skill," says Abraham M. Rosenthal, young metropolitan editor of *The New York Times,* whose own writing brought him a Pulitzer Prize for foreign correspondence. "Writing skill not only in news, but also in magazine articles and books.

"When a job applicant tells me he has been covering say, politics for the *Milwaukee Journal,* I want to see not only clippings of his political stories, but whatever else he has written on any subject anywhere, even what he failed to get printed. If he has done nothing else, I'm not interested in him, no matter how good a political reporter he was."

When the authors were your age, serious newspapers, in reaction against "sob sister" technique of the then new tabloids, cultivated a gray objectivity. Currently there is a swing back to writing "with heart" or with humor, as the occasion may require.

Tom Wolfe of the *New York Herald Tribune* made an instant reputation with his highly individual style. Sent by his paper to cover a hot-rod auto show, Wolfe came back with this:

"Here were all these . . . *weird* . . . nutty-looking, crazy, baroque, custom cars, sitting in little nests of pink angora angel's hair."

Far from getting him fired, that wild prose got him an assignment from *Esquire* to cover an auto show in Los Angeles. This time Wolfe went further out: "There Goes (Varoom! Varoom!) That Kandy-Kolored, Tangerine-Flake, Streamline Baby." From then on, he was in, man!

You will not be expected to cultivate a style as exotic as Wolfe's, but you will be expected to write clearly and vividly.

CURIOSITY

When Alice saw the White Rabbit with the watch scamper by, she followed him right down the hole to find out what he was in such a hurry about. She had a "nose for news," the instinct of a reporter. Poking his nose into other people's business is the way a reporter minds his own business. "Curiosity" is the word editors use when asked what is the most important trait for a newsman to have.

"He should be consumed by curiosity about everything under the sun and beyond," says Turner Catledge, executive editor of *The New York Times*. "There isn't a damn thing he sees or hears that wouldn't make an interesting story. If he merely walks out of the office to the elevator, he will notice something that might make a story. He wants to dig it out; then he has an irresistable desire to tattle, to tell the world all about it."

Perhaps you have heard the old joke about the cub reporter who came back from a society wedding with no story because the bride did not show up! The first rule a reporter learns is that there is *always* a story, if he is alert enough to spot it and persistent enough to pry it out.

The late Meyer Berger, one of the great reporters of our time, had a superlative gift of curiosity. Here is a typical example:

He was doing a feature story about the Tombs, the antiquated New York City prison that was soon to be demolished. In the men's room, he noticed a dusty parcel on a high shelf. Rummaging in the package, Mike found some polished wooden staves with red velvet handles and tassels.

"What's this?" he asked the warden.

"Damned if I know," the warden said. "Never saw them before."

Then, going to the files of a historical museum, Mike discovered an old engraving showing warders carrying those ceremonial batons while escorting a prisoner to the gallows in the courtyard of the Tombs. The sticks had lain unnoticed in the john since the last hanging fifty years before. By simply bothering to look, Mike got a colorful lead for his story.

TRUTH AND OBJECTIVITY

Striving to discover the truth and make it known gives the newsman a unique mission.

"The reporter," as Joseph and Stewart Alsop put it in one of their syndicated columns, "is the people's eyes and ears."

The newsman's primary duty is to bring the people the truth regardless of whom it helps or hurts. This is a large order.

You may have heard people say, "You can't believe what you read in the newspapers."

It must be admitted that the press does not carry out its duty perfectly, frequently not even well. The whole truth and nothing but the truth is not always presented in sensitive matters of race, religion, politics. But that only proves there are timid, prejudiced, and cynical men in journalism as in other professions. The ideal remains.

As it is, the American people have the fullest and most outspoken press on earth, despite its many faults.

Many laymen seem to believe that journalists must make the facts conform to their publisher's policy whether the truth is served or not.

The fact is that in the great majority of reporting and editing jobs, the publisher's policy concerns you not at all. All that will be required of you is accuracy, objectivity, fairness. In thirty years of work for newspapers and magazines, neither of the authors of this book was ever ordered to write a lie or omit the truth.

For key positions where policy is expressed, the publisher

chooses, of course, men of sympathetic views. You can cross or blow up that bridge when you come to it, which will probably not be for some years.

Make up your mind now that as a journalist you are going to be completely honest. That is not to say you may expect to write just as you please. You will have to carry out the assignment, suppressing your prejudices and preferences, able to see faults in your saints, give devils their due.

As a newsman you must try to take an objective attitude. Always a nonpartisan observer, you must seek all the facts and reveal them regardless of their effect. While you may cherish your opinions, you must keep them out of your work. The editor will not ask whether you are a Christian or an atheist before he assigns you to cover Billy Graham's revival; and he will expect a fair account of a Barry Goldwater speech even if you are a liberal Democrat.

AGGRESSIVENESS

Editors demand aggressiveness in going after a story. The good reporter never takes "no comment" for an answer, though he hears it often. He persists endlessly; if one source remains sealed, he tries another and another until he cracks the story.

Thirty-five-year-old Gene Goltz of the *Houston Post* dug up evidence of corruption in Pasadena, Texas, that led to the indictment of the mayor and other officials. He persevered for months, though he was beaten, had his nose broken, and his life threatened.

Going after news, reporters have shown zeal others would call excessive. They have sneaked into private meetings, called people at 2:00 A.M. to question them, posed as convicts or mental patients to gather facts, all in the public interest.

For six months, Edgar May of the *Buffalo Evening News* worked as a welfare case investigator to amass material exposing abuses and inefficiency in the county welfare system. Only his managing editor knew why he had "disappeared." His series of fourteen articles sparked a thorough reform.

Being aggressive does not mean being a bully, rude, or a pest.

Most reporters today are polite, even pleasant. They get information by winning the confidence, the friendly cooperation of people. One of the shyest of girl reporters got an intimate, exclusive story from a gangster's "moll" by her sympathetic, innocent, gentle manner.

WORK UNDER PRESSURE

Newswork is often called a young man's business, which means that it takes a lot out of you. You have to be able to work fast, under pressure, sometimes in highly uncomfortable and distracting conditions. You seldom have peace and quiet to think or time to rework an article.

Reporters customarily have only just enough time to write a story once, as fast as they can hit the typewriter keys. They have typed a story on their knees in a jolting bus, or scribbled notes under fire in a foxhole, or dictated ad lib from a glass telephone booth while a riot raged outside. And they are not forgiven omissions or errors because they were nervous or didn't have time to check!

The closer the deadline, the greater the pressure. Ordinarily, you have to work faster on a weekly than a monthly, on a daily than a weekly, and for a wire service fastest of all.

Among the 1,700 newspapers and 4,000 radio stations served by The Associated Press, for instance, one has a deadline every minute. The A.P. reporter may have to telephone additions to his running story every ten minutes. Back in the office, a re-writeman may have to pound out more copy in one seven-hour workday than you write in a whole school year, and do it at the rate of one page in five minutes.

A newspaper copyreader often must edit at scanning speed, sending the copy to the composing room one paragraph at a time and writing the headline from notes later.

JUDGMENT AND BACKGROUND

Accurate, snap judgment as to the relative importance of assorted facts, perception to hit the bull's-eye in rapid fire question and statement, is probably innate. People born without it do not make good reporters or editors.

Even with good, quick judgment, you cannot function in journalism without what editors call "background." That is not innate, of course, but built up by reading, memorizing a mass of information useful to your work—names, titles, events, everything pertaining to current affairs. You cannot deal with what's new unless you know what's old.

It is not too soon to begin building your background right now in preparation for your first job. It is gained by reading the newspapers thoroughly every day and devouring also the weekly news reviews, informative magazines, books on current topics.

"It is amazing how few kids who come to me for jobs read the papers," David Starr, executive editor of the *Long Island Daily Press*, complains. "I always bring up a current event to test their knowledge. If they are not interested enough to read the paper, I am not interested in them."

OTHER QUALITIES

Among other qualities editors look for are appetite for hard work, responsibility and initiative in working alone, ability to cultivate news sources.

But, perhaps the greatest quality of all is love, love of the work in spite of all its shortcomings.

"I wouldn't exchange jobs with any titan or tycoon in the land," says Bob Considine, roving columnist for King Features. "Gathering, phrasing and dispensing news and ideas is the world's most enchanting job."

Journalism will not be worth doing if you don't love it more than anything else.

Chapter Six | EDUCATION FOR A CAREER IN JOURNALISM

To understand and translate into clear, laymen's terms the complexities of international politics, technicalities of economics and finance, mysteries of science, gobbledegook of sociology demands a very broad education, indeed.

Newsmen of today are much better educated than those of only one generation ago.

"I could not get a job as a beginner today on *The New York Times,*" boasts its executive editor, Turner Catledge. "I don't have enough education."

Although there have been in the recent past some great reporters who never finished high school (Mike Berger and David Brinkley are among them), about 80 percent of newsmen today are college alumni.

While a Phi Beta Kappa key is not mandatory for employment nowadays, a college diploma definitely is required of a beginner on a metropolitan newspaper, a national magazine, or a large radio or television station. Even the copyboys in the top companies have bachelor's degrees, not uncommonly master's. You don't have a prayer of meeting the competition for the best beginners' jobs without a college education.

LIBERAL ARTS OR JOURNALISM?

What kind of college education should you choose, straight liberal arts or journalism school?

Journalism courses were introduced about sixty years ago to

upgrade the quality of recruits to newspaper work. Controversy about their value has been going on ever since.

Proponents argue that journalism courses help a student to test his fitness for the field in general and select his specialty, that since vocational skill must be learned either on the job or in school, why not in school?

"Besides," says the American Council on Education for Journalism, "a journalism diploma insures a job. . . .

"More and more employers are seeking journalism graduates. They find in these young people an alertness, ambition, and capacity for performance with a minimum of training and coaching."

The opposition among educators argues that journalism does not require professional study on the college level. Many of the best institutions, such as Harvard, Yale, Princeton, Amherst, Williams, Radcliffe, Bryn Mawr, give no journalism courses. Many editors maintain no time should be subtracted from cultural study to learn vocational skills.

"We can teach journalism, but we are not equipped to give a college education," asserts Norman E. Isaacs, executive editor of the *Louisville Courier-Journal*. "We frown on undergraduate journalism courses."

Among broadcasting executives, journalism courses have won less acceptance than among newspaper editors. Lowell Thomas voices their view:

"If I planned a career in journalism today, I would skip all the vocational courses and concentrate on the classics, history, English literature, some science. . . . I'd take one foreign language right from kindergarten and another later, philosophy, logic and political science. . . . If you expect to spend your life before a microphone, devote some time to public speaking. . . ."

So the debate goes on. However, everyone is agreed in recommending the broadest cultural curriculum, whether or not journalism courses are taken in addition. The American Council on Education for Journalism itself insists that at least three-fourths of the four-year college program be taken in liberal arts, no more than one-fourth in journalism. And virtually nobody objects to a one year graduate course in journalism following a four year, straight, liberal arts degree.

Indeed, many editors prefer it.

"The best for us," says Mr. Isaacs, "is a good liberal arts degree plus a master's at a top J-school like Columbia's."

Surveys by The Newspaper Fund indicate that graduates with master's degrees get better jobs than those with bachelor's degrees and at higher salaries.

Altogether, more than 19,000 students, about 64 percent men, were taking majors in journalism in 1965-66, a record number. About 90 percent were undergraduate students. Most of the remaining 10 percent were taking master's degrees. The few going for a Ph.D. were preparing to teach college journalism or to become professional researchers in marketing analysis for the mass communications media.

WHAT COURSES TO TAKE

The A.C.E.J. recommends among the cultural courses, English composition, American and English literature, foreign languages, history, political science, economics, philosophy, psychology, science, and social sciences.

Survey courses will be of more use to a journalist than narrowly specialized studies; for instance, the history of philosophy rather than a semester in Immanuel Kant alone, general biology rather than a laboratory course in invertebrate zoology.

If you have already selected a field you intend to specialize in, take courses that will prepare you for it.

To be a foreign correspondent, you must master thoroughly at least one foreign language. French is the most widely useful, German next. There is a great shortage of newsmen fluent in Russian or the oriental languages.

There is a demand for science writers, but the field has grown so big and complex, you may have to specialize in the physical or biological or behavioral sciences.

Religion is a journalistic specialty that is growing, both in the religious press and in the general press. If your interest lies in that direction, take courses in comparative religion and the history of religion.

If you wish to become an education editor, take some courses in history of education and modern teaching methods.

HOW TO CHOOSE A JOURNALISM COLLEGE

To help you select a college in which to study journalism, there are listed in the Appendix forty-seven schools or departments of journalism in the United States that are accredited by the American Council on Education for Journalism as meeting its standards. All these give bachelor's and graduate degrees, except Columbia, which is a graduate school only. The bachelor's degree requires four years, the master's one year more, the doctorate usually two years beyond that.

Also listed are 103 other colleges offering either degrees or majors in journalism.

Lack of accreditation by the A.C.E.J. is not necessarily a reflection on the quality of the teaching; it may be merely that the program is not extensive enough.

Student enrollment, varying from 500 to 25 at each college, is no indication of excellence either; some of the best schools are small.

The "sequences," or areas of study, are given for each school. More students are enrolled in the news-editorial sequence than in any other.

Opportunities for studying broadcast journalism are on the increase—126 schools offer a bachelor's degree in broadcasting, one, the master's only, 60 both bachelor's and master's degrees, and 17 the doctorate. There are 50 schools offering five semester hours or eight quarter-hours of broadcasting that do not lead to a degree.

In accredited colleges, journalism courses are not usually given before the junior year. Spread over one or two years, these total about thirty credit hours. All journalism majors are required to take basic reporting and editing techniques, as well as the theory, history and responsibility of mass communications.

In a typical, basic workshop course, the students are organized

TV CLASS: Students learn technique in journalism school by actual news broadcasting. (*Columbia School of Journalism*)

like the city staff of a newspaper. A student city editor makes assignments from the wire-service ticker, the morning paper, and his own ideas. Student reporters go out on actual stories, returning to write them for the deadline.

Their copy, as well as the regular wire-service copy, is edited by student copyreaders, who also write the headlines. Students make up Page One, and perhaps some other pages as well, from the copy in hand.

A few schools have a typographical lab that can set a token amount of copy in type and print it.

In the workshop, instructors advise, but do not direct, the

student staff. Afterward, the instructors guide a critique of the day's work, comparing it, when possible, to that of the professional newspapers in the same city.

The assignments as reporters, rewritemen, copyreaders, editors, and so forth are rotated among the students during the school year.

In addition, students take elective courses in subjects like magazine article writing and marketing, Washington and foreign correspondence, critical writing, science reporting, television script writing, radio-show directing, film cutting, speech, photo-journalism, and many more.

Effort is made to have all courses practical. Original reporting, rather than library research, is stressed. In the broadcast courses, actual equipment is used and programs are broadcast from the college station. The photo-journalism courses include use of the camera, developing and printing pictures.

It is important to select a journalism school with the right orientation for you—which you can discover by scrutinizing the catalogue or writing to the dean.

Columbia, for instance, is daily newspaper oriented. Syracuse has a strong magazine department and also courses in religious journalism. Iowa meets the needs of the Midwest with courses in agricultural and community journalism, weekly newspaper management, home economics reporting. New York University is strong in public relations and house-organ journalism.

SCHOLARSHIPS

For journalism students there are scholarships worth more than $700,000. The Journalism Scholarship Guide, published annually, lists more than 1,000 totaling nearly $450,000 for undergraduates, and more than 150 graduate grants totaling about $270,000. These are in addition to the millions of dollars in aid available to college students in general.

HIGH SCHOOL PREPARATION

The foundation for a career in journalism can begin in high school, for the courses in English composition, modern history, and social sciences will prove valuable later on. High school is also a good place to acquire touch-typing and shorthand. A basic knowledge of photography is helpful also.

The high school student should try to attend one of the short summer courses, workshops, and seminars held for high school journalists at various colleges and universities across the country. More than sixty, most of one or two weeks, are described in the annual directory issue of *The Journalism Educator*.

GETTING EXPERIENCE

Employers prefer applicants to have not only a good general education but also some experience in journalism. How is an absolute beginner to get experience?

One of the best ways is to serve as your college's correspondent for a "downtown" newspaper. Every daily paper has a student correspondent at each college in its area. Some metropolitan papers have them at all the leading colleges. This part-time job may pay low space rates, a small retainer, or nothing, but it affords a chance to impress an editor with your ambition and talent. In any case, it will provide clippings to show a potential employer later. Some of our best newsmen got their start as campus correspondents.

If you can't make a connection with an outside paper, go out for your college paper. It is a good idea to work for the school paper even in high school. Your future employer will be pleased to see this evidence of early intention. Save your clippings!

Some journalism schools provide opportunities for their students to get experience while going to college. Some, like Michigan, assign their students to put out the campus newspapers. A few, like Missouri and Iowa universities and South Dakota State College, have journalism students produce community newspapers. Others, like Medill School of Journalism at Northwestern University, have seniors and graduate students work part time in Chicago newspapers, news services, magazines, and radio stations.

At least ninety-six journalism schools offer opportunities for pre-graduation experience by providing summer internships.

Such interneships gave more than one thousand temporary jobs last year, most of them in daily newspaper newsrooms, but some also in radio stations and on magazines. Some interneships earn credit toward a degree; some pay no money, others only expenses, while still others pay standard wages, up to $100 a week. The Newspaper Fund Inc., a pioneer force in internship, placed 114 students from liberal arts colleges on 108 papers in twenty-eight states last year and gave each a $500 scholarship toward the following year's tuition.

Interneships are not copyboy or clerk's jobs, but positions as cub reporters or copyreader trainees. The best internes may expect permanent jobs; the others recommendations to lesser employers.

ON-THE-JOB TRAINING

At least forty newspapers in more than half the states have formal, on-the-job training programs for beginners.

The *Wall Street Journal,* founder of the Newspaper Fund, puts trainees on its eight editions in as many cities at $100 a week. The Gannett chain, with headquarters in Rochester, New York, has an elaborate twenty-one-week course with required reading. The Copley chain takes ten youths from Pacific and Midwest campuses each year for training on its *San Diego Union.* The Knight papers farm out beginners to two Florida weeklies for training under semi-retired veteran editors.

The *Washington Star, Washington Post* and *New York Daily News* have notable training programs for reporter-candidates.

That of the *News* is particularly impressive. All fifty of its copyboys get a six months' trial as reporter-trainees. The trainee works four days a week as copyboy and one day as a cub reporter, covering actual stories, rewriting, and copyreading. His work may not be published, but it is criticized by an editor in charge of instruction. At the end of the period, the most promising—about five boys a year—are hired as cub reporters. The rest are offered jobs in other departments of the *News* or on lesser papers, or helped to find jobs in another business.

The *Nashville Tennessean* gives part-time copyboy jobs and

training to needy high school and college students while they are in school.

"Within six months, boys who are good prospects will show an interest by bringing in news tips or stories or pulling up to the copydesk when there's an empty chair," reports G. W. Churchill, executive assistant to the publisher. "This program was started about six years ago. Today better than half our top reporters are men who earned part of their way through school by working as copyboys at this paper."

FOR MORE INFORMATION

BOOKLETS, PAMPHLETS, PERIODICALS

Cost of Four Years of College. New York Life Insurance Company, Career Information Service, Box 51, Madison Square Station, New York, N.Y. Free. Gives tuition, cost of room and board at many colleges in U.S. and Canada.

Financial Aid for College Students. Financial Aid Branch, Division of Higher Education, Office of Education, U.S. Department of Health, Education, and Welfare, Washington 25, D.C. $1.25. Available from U.S. Printing Office, Washington, D.C.

Journalism Scholarship Guide. The Newspaper Fund, 44 Broad St., New York, N.Y. Free. Lists 1,000 undergraduate scholarships worth $400,000 for journalism students, and 160 fellowships for graduate journalism students worth $270,000.

Need a Lift to Educational Opportunities? Education and Scholarship Program, Americanism Division, American Legion, Indianapolis, Ind. Free. List of Legion scholarships.

Programs in Journalism. American Council on Education for Journalism, Ernie Pyle Hall, University of Indiana, Bloomington, Ind. Free. Lists schools with courses accredited by A.C.E.J.

Public Relations Education in American Colleges and Universities. Public Relations Society of America, 845 Third Ave., New York, N.Y. Free. Lists more than 300 schools offering courses in P.R.

Radio-Television Degree Programs in American Colleges and Universities. National Association of Broadcasters, 1771 N. St., N.W., Washington, D.C. Free. Covers 127 colleges offering education in broadcasting, though not only broadcast journalism.

Student Aid Annual and *Student Aid Bulletin.* Chronicle Guidance Publications Inc. Moravia, N.Y.

The Journalism Educator. Annual Directory Issue. American Society of Journalism School Administrators, Duquesne University, Department of Journalism, Pittsburgh, Pa. $2. Describes more than 140 schools and departments of journalism, also summer courses, workshops, seminars for journalism students, journalistic societies, etc.

The Journalism Quarterly. Association for Education in Journalism, University of Minnesota, School of Journalism, Minneapolis 14, Minn. Scholarly research articles.

REFERENCE BOOKS ON EDUCATION AND SCHOLARSHIPS

Lovejoy, Clarence J. *Lovejoy's College Guide*. New York: Simon & Schuster. Standard work; description of colleges in U.S. with costs. $6.50. Paper $3.50.

Lovejoy-Jones College Scholarship Guide. New York: Simon & Schuster. Lists college scholarships available in U.S. $4.95. Paper $2.95,

Lovejoy's Vocational School Guide. New York: Simon & Schuster. $5.95. Paper $2.95.

Scholarships, Fellowships and Loans. Cambridge, Mass.: Bellman Publishing Company.

Turner, D. B. and Tarr, H. A. *You Can Win a Scholarship!* New York: Arco Publishing Company. How to get a scholarship to college.

SCHOLARSHIP AID FOR NEGROES

National Negro Scholarship Fund and Service for Negro Students. 6 East 82nd St., New York, N.Y.

ORGANIZATIONS FOR HIGH SCHOOL AND COLLEGE JOURNALISTS

Associated Collegiate Press. Critical analyses for college papers, magazines, yearbooks. Annual convention with short courses for student staffs. Publishes *Business Review* monthly; *News and Feature Service* weekly. 18 Journalism Bldg., University of Minnesota, Minneapolis 14, Minn.

Catholic School Press Association. For staffs and advisers of Catholic secondary school and college publications. Biennial convention. College of Journalism, Marquette University, Milwaukee 3, Wis. Publishes *Catholic School Editor*.

Columbia Scholastic Press Association. Gives advice and help with student publications at all levels from elementary school through college. Annual conference in October. Annual convention in March for editors and advisers. Low Memorial Library, Columbia University, New York 27, N.Y. Publishes *School Press Review* monthly.

Future Journalists of America. National Headquarters, University of

Oklahoma, Norman, Okla. National society for high school students.

National Scholastic Press Association. Advises and helps with high school papers and magazines. Annual convention and clinic for student staffs. 18 Journalism Bldg., University of Minnesota, Minneapolis 14, Minn. Publishes *Scholastic Editor* monthly.

Pacific Slope School Press. Regional association for high school publications in eight Western states. Annual clinic. 118 Communications Bldg., University of Washington, Seattle 5, Wash.

Quill and Scroll Society. Chapters in more than 8,600 high schools in U.S. National Headquarters, School of Journalism, State University of Iowa, Iowa City, Iowa. Publishes *Quill and Scroll* bimonthly.

COLLEGE JOURNALISTIC FRATERNITIES

Among almost a dozen of these, the principal ones are:

Sigma Delta Chi. For men, with 88 undergraduate and 81 professional chapters throughout U.S. Publishes *The Quill* monthly. National Headquarters, 35 East Wacker Dr., Chicago, Ill.

Theta Sigma Phi. For women, with undergraduate and professional chapters throughout U.S. Publishes *The Matrix*. National Headquarters, 1018 West 11th St., Austin, Texas.

2

NEWSPAPERS AND WIRE SERVICES

Chapter Seven

WHEN BIG NEWS BREAKS

At 5:27 on a Tuesday evening in November, the power failed in New York City and, about the same time, over most of north-eastern United States. Millions of people were marooned high in office buildings, in blacked-out factories, stuck in subways and elevators. For them there was nothing to do but try to get home through the dark streets.

For the staff of *The New York Times* it was a call to emergency duty. The blackout was news and therefore must be covered and told.

Of course, the paper, like everything else, was crippled. It had no lights; its news tickers, typesetting machines, and presses were dead; the telegraph and cable services, which ordinarily bring in hundreds of thousands of words of news daily, were knocked out. Only the telephones worked, and they were soon jammed with calls.

But the paper's disablement was another challenge to the newsmen. Clerks went scurrying to buy all the flashlights in Times Square stores, all the candles in Woolworth's, all the banquet candles from nearby hotels; a resourceful Irish circulation man mooched the votive candles from neighborhood Catholic churches. Soon the big newsroom was working again in the flickering golden light.

The city editor assigned thirty-five reporters and rewritemen to the blackout story. Other news from the rest of the country and from overseas was telephoned in constantly by correspondents outside the blacked-out area. Reporters, secretaries, clerks, anybody who could type was dragooned into taking down this flood of spoken words.

The mechanical problem was harder to lick. New Jersey had escaped the blackout, and the *Newark Evening News* offered to lend *The Times* its printing facilities and men until seven o'clock next morning, when its own first edition would have to go to press.

A *Times* staff-in-exile of twenty men—including copyboys, rewritemen, copyreaders, makeup men, and news editors—were shipped to Newark in one delivery truck. The *News* staff made room for them in a corner of their city room, and both staffs worked independently side by side. *Times* photographs were printed in the *News* lab. In the composing room, *News* printers concentrated on *The Times* copy first.

Television crews barged in to film the scene; a *News* reporter said, "It's like Hollywood here!"

Meanwhile, most of the copy was still being produced in the Times Square office. An impromptu courier service of men in cars and on motorcycles kept running it to Newark, a hair-raising, forty-minute trip in the dark.

By 1:00 A.M., *The Times* reporters and editors had got up enough copy and pictures to fill a paper of ten pages, instead of the ninety-six scheduled before the blackout. All ads were omitted.

But overcrowding and confusion in the *Newark News* composing room delayed printing for several hours. When the presses finally began to roll at 4:11 A.M., the exhausted crews cheered. The seven o'clock deadline stopped the run at 480,000 copies.

That was only about half of normal, but *The New York Times* was the only morning paper in New York to appear that day. Most of the staff slept for a few hours wherever they could in the office and then went back to work on the next day's paper.

This is an example of newspaper journalism at its best. Since the daily newspaper is the foundation of all journalism, let us look at the organization of a typical newspaper.

THE NEWSROOM

The heart of the news operation is the newsroom, or city room to use an older term. Unlike the conventional business office, it is one, large, open floor characteristically untidy; littered with paper; bare of rugs, pictures, comfortable furniture.

In that big, open space, from thirty to three hundred men and women (depending on the size of the local staff) may work. Only the managing editor has a private office. Everybody else must concentrate on his job despite clacking typewriters, ringing telephones, conversations of others. Though it seems impossible, you do get used to it.

The atmosphere is marked by shirt-sleeved informality, a universal, first-name friendliness. When not busy, reporters write letters, free-lance articles or novels, read, spin yarns, even play cards—which always astonishes visitors.

"More like a club than a business office," a Swedish newspaperman exclaimed in delight on his first visit to New York.

Most of the room is occupied by the writers' typewriter desks, jammed together, row on row, with a telephone on each or on every second one. If the paper is large enough to have sub-departments for sports, women's news, financial news, and so forth, these writers are usually grouped at the rear, sometimes each group enclosed by a fence or glass partition.

The city editor (called metropolitan editor on some papers), surrounded by his assistants, sits up front in a spot from which he can command his men.

Beyond him are the arc-shaped copydesks on which writers' stories are edited. In close touch with their copyreaders are the national and foreign editors.

Railed off in a corner is the "bullpen," stamping ground of the news editor and his assistants.

Either in an enclosed cubby or in an adjacent wire room, the teletypes of the wire services are ceaselessly clattering. Big newspapers have a dozen or more of these news tickers. When big news breaks, each machine peals a series of warning bells.

WIRE ROOM: Teletypes of a dozen press services are clattering out news around the clock. (*The New York Times*)

THE NEWS OPERATION

The news operation goes on anywhere from eighteen to twenty-four hours a day.

On an afternoon paper, the first or "lobster" shift comes on about midnight to get up copy for the "bulldog," or first edition. Some afternoon papers go to press as early as 7:00 A.M., others not until noon. The bulk of the staff works from 8:00 A.M to 3:00 or 4:00 P.M. The final edition goes to bed ordinarily before 5:00

COMPOSITOR: On the stone, printer puts galleys (columns) of type into page forms according to diagrams drawn by makeup editors. (*The New York Times*)

PRESSROOM: Each newspaper page is cast as half-cylinder plate of metal (stacks at left) and bolted around rollers in presses. (*The New York Times*)

P.M. Only a skeleton crew to cover night assignments remains on duty after that hour.

On a morning paper, the "day side" arrives between 10:00 A.M. and 1:00 P.M, the "night side" between 1:00 and 8:00 P.M. The peak number of men is at work about 6:00 P.M, generally tapering off until "goodnight" about 4:00 A.M. The first edition closes about 9:00 P.M. and the last at 4:00 A.M., although emergencies will call forth an extra anytime up to 8:00 A.M.

Within this wide span of working time, each newspaperman puts in ordinarily seven hours a day, although he frequently works overtime.

A big newspaper may receive from its reporters, wire services, and press agents more than a million words of news a day. From this perhaps not more than 200,000 can be printed.

After the selected stories are written, edited, and headlined, they are carried by conveyor belt or pneumatic tube to the composing room. There they are set into type on linotype machines operated either by printers or by electronic computers. On long counters called "stones," compositors arrange the galleys (columns) of type in page forms. From the full forms, papier-mâché molds called matrices are made. From the "mats" stereotypers cast metal, half-cylindrical plates that are clamped around rollers on the rotary presses, each of which automatically prints, cuts, folds, and counts 50,000 papers an hour.

Chapter Eight

WHAT NEWSPAPERMEN DO —THE WRITERS

REPORTERS

Outsiders tend to use the words "newspaperman" and "reporter" as synonyms. Actually only five-sevenths of the newspaper journalists in the United States are reporters—about 25,000 men and women.

Ordinarily, each reporter does the whole job on his story himself—getting the facts, checking, writing. Nevertheless, editors tend to think of their reporters as either "diggers" or "writers" because most men are better at one task than the other.

Ed Mowery, for the *New York World-Telegram and Sun,* dug five years for evidence that cleared Louis Hoffner, a clerk, of a holdup murder he did not commit but for which he served twelve years in prison.

One of the greatest writers among newspaper reporters was Ernie Pyle, World War II correspondent, who was killed in the Pacific. Here is an excerpt from his classic newspaper account of an American infantry unit in central Italy.

Dead men had been coming down the mountain all evening lashed onto the backs of mules. They came lying belly-down across wooden pack saddles, their heads hanging down on one side, their stiffened legs sticking out from the other, bobbing up and down as the mules walked. . . .

"This one is Captain Waskow," one of the soldiers said quietly.

Two men unlashed his body from the mule and lifted it

off and laid it in the shadow beside the stone wall. The men in the road stood around and gradually I could sense them moving close to Captain Waskow's body. Not so much to look as to say something in finality to him and to themselves.

One soldier came and said out loud, "God damn it!" and then he walked away. Then a soldier came and stood beside the officer and bent over and he, too, spoke to his dead captain, and he said, "I sure am sorry, sir." Then the first man squatted down and took the captain's hand and sat there holding the dead hand in his own and never uttered a sound all the time.

The rest of us went back into the cowshed, leaving the five dead men in a line, end to end, in the shadow of the wall. We lay down on the straw and pretty soon we were all asleep.

No matter how beautifully you can write, do not expect that as a cub reporter you will be sent out as a war correspondent. Cubs are started on the local staff, sometimes called the city, or metropolitan, staff.

Since local news is covered more intensively than any other, the local staff includes the majority of any newspaper's reporters. They cover beats or general assignments or specialties.

BEAT MEN

A beat is any fixed source of daily, usually official, news, such as Police Headquarters, City Hall, the courts, a government bureau, the United Nations, and so on.

Let us say, for example, you are assigned to cover the municipal office building. You go there every morning directly from home, meeting your competitors from rival papers in the pressroom provided by the city and equipped with telephones and typewriters. On the calendar of the day's events, the most important item you see is a public hearing on new city sales taxes. You check in by telephone with your city editor, who assigns you to the hearing. It goes without saying that you are also responsible for picking up any other news that may turn up on your beat.

At the hearing, you sit at a press table with the other reporters, taking notes on anything newsworthy. If you are on an afternoon paper, you will have to leave three or four times during the day to telephone the facts to a rewriteman who will write a "running story" that changes for each edition. If you are on a morning paper, you have time to sit the hearing out.

After the hearing ends, you may find in the pressroom mimeographed news releases from press officers of various city departments. It is likely these are routine matters requiring little or no investigation.

You go off alone to chat with the Park Commissioner about a rumor that a millionaire has offered to donate a public café to a city park. The commissioner confirms it. He is willing to give you the details and an architect's rendering of the building, but "please don't quote me," he says. You are free to print the facts but not to ascribe them, or any opinion of them, to him.

When the municipal offices close in late afternoon, you take all your material to your newspaper office. You report to your city editor, who tells you how much space to give each story. Before you begin writing, you consult clippings in the "morgue" for background and to check details of persons and matters involved.

On a morning paper, you will write your stories with the time element "yesterday." On an afternoon paper, you are also writing for tomorrow, the bulldog edition, since today's press run is finished, but you will avoid "yesterday." You will write something like, "the Park Commissioner is considering . . ."

You may also be ordered to write an "overnight" on the tax hearing; that is, a story reviewing all the facts reported in today's paper but printed tomorrow under an updated lead, such as, "City authorities were studying today new proposals for sales taxes. . . ."

Next morning, you are delighted and your rivals are chagrined to see your exclusive story on the park café on Page One.

In the seventy-five cities with competing newspapers, a beat man faces a dilemma about cooperating with his rivals. If you share your exclusives with them, you will not advance yourself. If you do not, you will be beaten by them occasionally, and personal relations may get frosty. Ask your city editor for guidance on this problem.

GENERAL ASSIGNMENT REPORTERS

The better reporters on the local staff are usually put on general assignments or specialties.

Most days, general assignment men arrive for work not knowing what they are going to do. But news is bound to happen every day in any town. A commuter train may jump the track, a psychopath commit murder in the subway, an opera star drop dead on stage, jewels be stolen from a museum, the president of a new republic arrive in town, Blue Cross demand higher premiums.

Things will occur out of town too: floods may drown Missouri River towns, the government may be overthrown in Guatemala, a Negro state senator may be denied his seat.

There can be, of course, no advance notice on spontaneous news breaks. On scheduled events, such as public meetings, conventions, conferences, editors will usually give reporters one or two days' notice.

General assignment reporters cover everything not handled by beat men, correspondents, or specialists. In emergencies, they augment or supersede the others. For instance, Martin Luther King's march in Alabama was covered not only by regional correspondents but also by general assignment men sent out from home offices. On national election campaigns every general assignment man will help cover politics.

It is constant variety that gives general assignments their great appeal. Active reporters like Homer Bigart travel the world, hardly ever doing the same thing twice. Another reporter we know has flown high above the Arctic to observe an eclipse of the sun, cruised on the sea bottom in a new submarine, interviewed a President, covered funerals of a millionaire and a Bohemian poet, fires, riots, murder trials, hurricanes, written sad stories about juvenile killers, humorous stories of political campaigns, harrowing accounts of plane crashes, ecstatic accounts of ski holidays, and tens of thousands more. And his career is not unusual.

A cub may be put on general assignments for diversified training. He must expect such apprentice jobs as covering civic association meetings, reporting church sermons, writing routine obituaries.

But no law confines him to such drab chores. He can make his own assignments. These will likely be features or investigations rather than hard news, but all the better to show off his writing skill. Permission to do each story must be obtained from the city editor, of course.

As a cub, Gay Talese was lost amid a galaxy of stars on the huge staff of *The New York Times*. Not content to wait years for good assignments, he roved the city on his own time, interviewing obscure people in characteristic jobs. His series of sketches made his name as a feature writer.

FEATURE WRITERS

Feature writers are general assignment reporters with particular skill at "color," or human interest, stories rather than "hard" news. Familiar examples of features are personality sketches, interviews, descriptions of life off the beaten track.

Sometimes, a feature writer is assigned to a "sidebar" to a big news story. In covering a tornado, say, one reporter may do the main news story, while a feature writer does an accessory story of vivid description and interviews with survivors. In the course of work, any good reporter may be required to do an occasional feature.

SPECIALISTS

As a journalism student, you will be advised to take a broad interest in everything, yet also to specialize. Despite the apparent contradiction, it is possible to do both—to take a general interest in news and a special interest in one subject.

There is no question that news staffs are growing increasingly

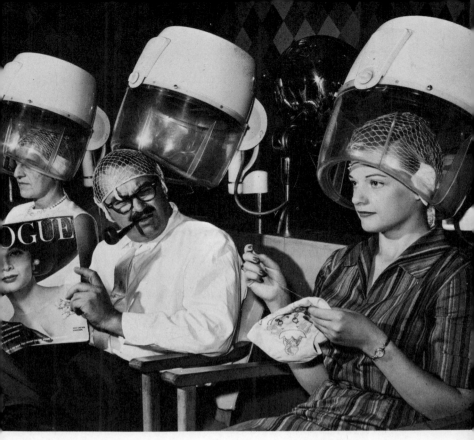

FEATURE WRITER: A male reporter investigates how the other half lives for humorous feature. (*Long Island Daily Press*)

departmentalized—the bigger the paper, the more departmentalization. Though there may be more fun on general assignments, there may be more opportunity in specialization. Big staffs have become collections of specialists. So few Page One general assignments are left after the foreign correspondents, Washington correspondents, and specialists are assigned, that two or three stars will monopolize them all.

Large staffs have sub-departments for sports, business and finance, society, women's news, and so on. There may be separate departments for the theater, movies, television, art, music, or instead, one "cultural news" department with specialists serving each Muse within it.

Even within each department, the writers may be specialized. For instance, some sports writers cover only baseball, one perhaps the Yankees alone, living with that team from spring training through the World Series. In business news, one man covers the stock market; another, real estate; a third, banks, and so on. In women's news, one girl covers fashions; another, child care; a third, food; a fourth, home furnishings.

On the general staff, directly under the city editor, work many specialists—in labor news, politics, education, urban renewal, social welfare, transportation, religion, science, military affairs, whatnot. Very large staffs have specialists within specialties. In politics, for example, there may be a specialist in municipal politics, another in state politics, and one or more in national politics. In science, one man may cover biological science; another, physical science; and a third, space exploration.

A news specialist may be said to be a beat reporter who covers an area of knowledge rather than a particular place. There are many areas, particularly in the sciences, social sciences, and industry, formerly the exclusive province of technical journals, that are scoured for news by newspapers today. The general public is better educated now and more curious about such things.

Technical knowledge is essential to reporting some news. For example, no reporter ignorant of chemistry and biology could exercise his own judgment on scores of research papers presented at an American Medical Association convention. Most science reporters have had educations in science, although, curiously, one of the most famous, William L. Laurence, who wrote the pool stories for the world press on the first atomic bomb in 1945, did not major in science when he went to Harvard.

Some specialists got their technical knowledge by practicing in the field before entering journalism. Virgil Thomson was a composer and musician before becoming a music critic; Hanson Baldwin, a Navy officer before becoming a military and naval writer. There are education editors who began as teachers, religion editors who were theological students, sports writers who are former golf or tennis champions.

However, most newspaper specialists are not qualified to practice in their fields. At best, they have had enough formal education in the subject to understand what the professionals are doing and saying. Many picked up all their knowledge as they covered stories in the area, learning as they went along.

When Lucy Freeman was reporting social welfare news, she noticed how often psychiatric care was needed but unavailable. At that time, she happened to be going through psychoanalysis herself. She began specializing in news of psychiatry, studying privately, and is now an outstanding lay writer on it.

The city editor depends upon specialists to discover news that would not otherwise come to his attention. That discovery comes from knowledge, daily concentration and personal contacts in the field.

The job of specialist also requires a sharp news sense and the skill to make technical things intelligible and interesting to the lay public. The specialist must be a newsman first and expert second. That is why the paper does not simply hire a doctor to cover medical news, a broker to report financial news, and so forth.

Specialization has its advantages. You are less subject to nuisance chores like routine obits, checking lists of names, covering two-alarm fires. You have more freedom in making your own assignments. On the whole, pay is better than on general assignments. It is pleasant to be a pundit, telling people what's what, making *Who's Who in America* writing magazine articles on your specialty.

Specialization has some disadvantages, too. You enjoy less variety than on general assignments. You will forfeit a chance to become the Number One reporter, who is always a general assignment man. You will also decrease your chance of becoming a top executive, because it is difficult for the managing editor to replace a good specialist.

If specialization appeals to you, begin preparing in college by taking appropriate courses. Among specialties in demand but in short supply at this moment are the sciences, particularly space, and, to a lesser degree, fine arts. In the field of foreign correspondence, there is a crying need for reporters fluent in the Cyrillic and oriental languages.

In sports, on the contrary, there is an abundance of specialists. Every American boy is an expert at some sport, and television is competing strongly with newspaper sports coverage. The key to success as a sports writer is a highly original, entertaining style. All the greatest had it—Grantland Rice, John Kieran, Damon Runyon, Paul Gallico, Red Smith. It is a rare gift. Before embarking on a career as sports specialist, think it over carefully.

REWRITEMEN

On a newspaper, a rewriteman is not a writer whose principal duty is to rework other reporters' stories to improve the prose. Once in a while, he may have to do that.

Most of the time, his work is to write stories from facts given him over the telephone by reporters in the field; to do his own reporting by telephone; to write news stories from texts of speeches, statements, press agents' releases sent into the office; to coordinate information from wire services and correspondents, and write a roundup story.

Some news stories are always handled by rewrite, like the weather, holiday traffic, election results, Christmas celebrations. In the course of their work, all reporters do some rewrite; the rewriteman is regularly assigned to it, not leaving his desk except in case of manpower shortage.

Rewritemen occupy the front row of reporters' desks, where the city editor can keep in close touch with them. Their telephones are equipped with headsets.

They must be fast, facile writers. The job can be nerve-wracking when a Page One story breaks just before deadline. We have seen a rewriteman turn out a great story of an air crash while three others, listening on telephones to reporters at the scene, shouted facts to him, and a copyboy kept zipping copy out of his typewriter one paragraph at a time.

Afternoon papers have comparatively large staffs of rewritemen. The lobster shift starts about midnight writing new leads on stories that have appeared in the morning papers. During the day the pressure on the rewritemen increases as they take stories over the telephone from reporters who have no time to come into the office.

On a morning paper, the day rewritemen start about 10:00 A.M. grinding out routine items on handouts sent in by press agents and taking stories on the telephone from part-time, out-of-town correspondents called "stringers."

The night rewritemen, coming on between 6:00 and 8:00 P.M., have a more exciting time handling late-breaking stories up to first-edition deadline. After the first edition is in, however, they usually have a respite, sitting out the "graveyard" watch until 4:00 A.M.—and in case of emergency until 7 A.M.

REWRITEMAN: He takes facts over the telephone from a reporter at the scene and writes the story. He must be a fast, facile writer. (*The New York Times*)

Virtually all rewritemen do general work. On large papers, sports and society news departments, the Washington bureau, and perhaps a large foreign bureau may have their own rewritemen. Special rewritemen to take stories from suburban correspondents are not uncommon. A few papers assign a rewriteman to the foreign desk to write "shirttails" (background and explanatory matter) to news bulletins from abroad. *The New York Times* has one rewriteman who does nothing but obituaries!

Only experienced reporters, though not the top, are assigned to rewrite. The Number One rewriteman may sit in occasionally for the city editor; he may win promotion to assistant city editor or even city editor.

CORRESPONDENTS

A correspondent is a reporter who works away from the town where the newspaper has its home office. All the stories you see in a paper under a place-name and dateline were sent by correspondents for the paper or a wire service.

Any newspaper's staff of full-time, salaried correspondents is always much smaller than its staff of local reporters. Staff correspondents may be stationed in the suburbs, in the state and national capitals, in other key cities of the country, and abroad.

A paper also has many "stringers," who are usually staff men on local papers and who serve as correspondents only on request and at space rates.

Foreign Correspondents   The foreign correspondent is the glamor boy of the newspaper business. In the movies, he is a trench-coated adventurer solving spy plots in Vienna and winning the beautiful blonde.

Well, there have indeed been some tall, dark, handsome correspondents; some who have delved into intrigues; and even one or two who have married the movie queen. But there are just as many who are middle-aged economics specialists with bifocals and a family.

If a good spy story turns up, any foreign correspondent jumps onto it, of course. Most of the time, however, he is concerned with the political and economic news of the country. He gets most of this information from the local press, government press officials, United States Embassy attachés, and such informed, unofficial acquaintances as he can cultivate.

In "closed" societies like the Soviet Union, it is difficult for him to get any facts outside the controlled press. And if he does manage to get any, he may not be allowed to send it through censorship or if he sneaks it through, he may get kicked out of the country.

To a great extent, the paper leaves it to its correspondent to decide what to cable. He tries to send one good story each day. If "hard" news is lacking, he falls back on "think pieces," his estimate of the situation from "informed sources." He also does features about the life of the country—for example, the plight of Negro intellectuals in South Africa, Castro's young Communists at work in Cuba, disappearance of the gondola from Venice, modernization of the geisha in Japan.

Thirty-five years ago, Walter Duranty blazed this trail by describing the everyday life of the Russian people rather than concentrating on the failures of communism. Today, every correspondent does that sort of thing everywhere. Obviously, it helps to speak the language, but few American correspondents in Africa, the Middle East, or Asia do.

Opportunity beckons those with a flair for exotic languages. Horace Greeley might advise today: "Go East, young man!"

The major bureaus are in the great capitals of the West—London, Paris, Rome, Berlin. Big papers keep more than one man in each—a bureau chief, a number of reporters, and bilingual aides. Those are the most desired posts, because the work is important, the living good, the local press competent and free, the language comprehensible, and English is widely understood. The jobs go to men of proven ability and service, never to beginners.

The young correspondent should not be shocked to find himself sent to Saigon, Jakarta, New Delhi, Léopoldville, or detailed to rove a huge, primitive area of Africa, the Middle East, or South America. Some spots average 100 degrees in winter and reek of human excrement.

DATELINE, KURDISTAN: Foreign correspondent interviews tribal elder on revolt against Iranian Government. (*The New York Times*)

Robert Alden, who has done time in nine countries of southeast Asia, defines a foreign correspondent as "just a reporter with amoebic dysentery."

Still, there are many young men eager to pack a bottle of paregoric in a flight bag and jet off to Outer Slobovia. Too many for the available posts. Few American newspapers maintain their own foreign correspondents; they get excellent coverage from the wire services and the best foreign journalists who act as stringers.

In peacetime, there are only about 250 American citizens serving as foreign correspondents for American newspapers. The *Journalism Quarterly* recently gave this table of papers with largest staffs: *The New York Times,* 45; *Christian Science Monitor,* 12; Fairchild papers, 12; *Chicago Tribune,* 11; *New York Herald Tribune,* 9; *Baltimore Sun* papers, 8; *Chicago Daily News, Wall Street Journal, Washington Post* and *Los Angeles Times,* 7 each.

Wartime doubles the number of American foreign correspondents. During World War II, a record total of 1,646 served overseas, though this number included those for all news media, not newspapers alone.

Not only in wartime, but also in peacetime, foreign correspondents are presumed on duty seven days a week, twenty-four hours a day. Any time they take off is at their risk of missing a story.

Jack James of United Press scooped the world on the outbreak of the Korean War on a dull Sunday when all his colleagues in Seoul took off on a picnic. Stopping at the United States Embassy to pick up his raincoat, James happened to overhear that North Korean troops had crossed into South Korea. His story was out before even our State Department at Washington had been informed.

The usual hitch of a foreign correspondent is three years, with one vacation of three months' home leave (round trip transportation for him and family paid) between hitches.

It is not every American who will like living and raising a family abroad. But for a single, adventurous man, it can be a fine life. He is a man of prestige in local circles; he lives first class on an expense account; he is his own boss and nearly every story he does lands on Page One.

Washington Correspondent   Many reporters consider Washington the best place for a newspaperman to work. It is certainly the richest source of important news for American newspapers. The task of Washington correspondents is to cover news of the national government. Other affairs in the district get scant attention.

Not every newspaper keeps a correspondent in Washington. Most depend upon the wire services. Some have only one to cover home-town Congressmen, and legislation and projects affecting the home area. Still others jointly retain one representative. The most important papers maintain large staffs in the capital, anywhere up to forty men and women.

The total Washington press corps of accredited correspondents numbers about twelve hundred.

Thirty or so have the White House beat, interrogating all visitors who see the President, picking up announcements from his press aides. They will keep vigil all night in times of emergency.

The President's most important statements, however, are made in person at press conferences either in the White House or in his executive office adjoining. These conferences are attended by hundreds of top newsmen of all media, including bureau chiefs, who vie in asking searching questions about the Administration's acts and policy.

About 250 newsmen have the Senate beat, an equal number the House of Representatives. The State Department and diplomatic agencies is one beat, the Attorney General and Supreme Court another, the Defense Department another, and so on through the long list.

One of the top beats is covering the President. That reporter will follow him anywhere, on trips to his Texas ranch, visits to New York, the hospital, abroad. The special press plane takes off just after the President's and lands just before it so reporters can observe him all the time he is on the ground.

Every job as Washington correspondent is a good one, and every correspondent a competent, experienced reporter.

The correspondent who covers the Treasury or Commerce Department, for instance, is the top economics writer for the paper; the correspondent who covers the Labor Department, the top labor reporter, who will be sent anywhere in the country to cover a big strike or labor convention.

The chief Washington correspondent is Number One reporter on the paper. He ranks a little below managing editor, whom he sometimes succeeds. He usually combines reportorial duties with executive tasks, although some papers relieve him of the latter with a bureau manager.

With so much high-class competition, Washington reporters vie

WASHINGTON CORRESPONDENTS: All top newsmen,
they hold jobs among the most interesting and important
in journalism. (*The New York Times*)

in cultivating confidential news sources who will leak exclusive
information to them. This tricky business requires particularly
good judgment. Interpretation is essential in Washington correspondence. The reporter must explain what a government action
means, as distinguished from what the official spokesmen say. To
interpret accurately without partisanship or editorializing takes
great skill that comes only with experience.

State Correspondents Metropolitan newspapers, and some big
community papers, keep one or more staff correspondents at the

state capital. The job of covering a state government is similar to that of covering the national government, though less specialized.

A lone correspondent will, of course, have to do everything himself. In a three-man bureau, say, the chief may cover the governor and executive departments, the second man, both houses of the legislature, and the third man, everything else. And everybody covers politics all the time, particularly if the governor happens to be a national figure, like Nelson Rockefeller, for instance.

A cub with an eye on becoming a political reporter should begin specializing in local politics on the city staff. After a few years of experience, he may be sent to the state capital, and after that to Washington. It helps if a politician he has been covering regularly moves up from a local to a state to a national post.

Regional Correspondents Big metropolitan newspapers have staff correspondents not only in the national and state capitals, but also in the great cities of the country: New York, Chicago, Los Angeles, Philadelphia, Detroit, Boston, Atlanta. New York is the most popular spot, of course—the majority of correspondents rent desks in *The New York Times*.

Relying heavily on the local press, the domestic correspondent looks for news of visitors from his home town and for other home angles. He may also send general news that is covered by the wire services, but he writes in the style and for the special interests of his paper. The correspondent must be able to work without supervision, and have had enough training on the home-town staff to know his paper's wants.

Some large papers also have staff correspondents roving regions of the country that make news. The most active area at this time is the South because of the struggle for racial integration there. A young, unmarried reporter has a good chance to get this job, because the work is hard, sometimes dangerous, and he must live out of a suitcase. It offers excellent experience and opportunity to prove his ability.

Suburban Beats Metropolitan papers have followed the movement of the middle-class population from the center of big cities to the suburbs by employing suburban staff correspondents. After a breaking-in period in the main office, cubs may be put out on suburban beats. They cover local news—civic association meetings, town boards, school boards, courts, police, society.

But it is small-town journalism really and can be discouraging. For if a candidate for President campaigns in your suburb, or a two-timing husband murders his wife, or a train wreck kills a hundred commuters, depend upon it, you will be superseded by a top man from the main office.

Covering a suburb as stringer for a metropolitan paper may, however, be a step toward a staff job in the big time. That opportunity is discussed in the section on community papers.

COLUMNISTS

A columnist is a writer never at loss for 600 or 700 interesting words. To keep up a high standard day after day for years grows stomach ulcers.

Columnists began their careers as reporters. The field is wide open to all reporters. All you have to do is show the kind of originality and cleverness that win widespread public applause. When your fan mail gets big enough you may, with luck, get a column of your own, with by-line and picture.

There are general interest columns of comment on all aspects of contemporary life, and specialized columns on politics, sports, society, the theater, fashions, hunting and fishing, nearly everything. Some columnists, like Jimmy Breslin and Bob Considine, occasionally cover a news story as a reporter, too.

When a column becomes popular enough, it is syndicated and the author, paid on royalty, may get rich.

The most widely syndicated Washington columnists have considerable influence on national affairs. Commentators like Walter Lippmann, Marquis Childs, David Lawrence, Drew Pearson, James Reston, the Alsop brothers, Roscoe Drummond are not so much reporters as critics who review politics as drama critics review plays.

In recent years, a lighter Washington columnist has appeared, satirists like Art Buchwald, Russell Baker, Arthur Hoppe, who lance politicians with ironical wit.

The columns by "trained seals," such as physicians on health, movie stars on beauty, clergymen on faith, are usually done by "ghosts"; that is, anonymous journalists employed by the signers and paid much, much less.

CRITICS

In the cultural centers—New York, Washington, Chicago, Boston, Philadelphia, San Francisco—newspapers employ full-time critics of drama, movies, music, art, books, television. In New York, especially, there are many critics in the various arts to review the great volume of new work.

The critics and specialist reporters also produce the section of reviews and news of the arts, which many metropolitan papers publish as a weekend supplement.

In general, however, papers require staff critics only for books, local movies, and television. Many use part-timers for this work. If an occasional play or art exhibition appears in town, they send a reporter who knows something about such things. Papers without staff critics depend upon wire services and syndicates for reviews of new work in all the arts.

The usual route to a critic's job is through reporting in the specialized field. That means, generally, a job in a large city where there is sufficient interest in the arts. It is possible for cubs with appropriate majors in college to start right out as a reporter in one of the arts departments. He does notes and news stories; then when there are too many openings for the regular critics to handle, he will get the least important one to review. After that, his progress depends upon his sharp critical judgment and clever writing style.

Ordinarily, the first critic is also head of his department. In large departments, he may be relieved of executive duties by a departmental editor or manager.

EDITORIAL WRITERS

It is traditional for newspapers to print from one to five editorials daily on the editorial page under the "masthead" (name, address, executives of the publishing company). These short articles of opinion are unsigned because they are supposed to represent the views, not of any individual, but of the "paper." There is a misconception among laymen that the paper's opinion is the consensus of an editorial board. This is almost never so. Almost invariably, the paper's policy is set by the publisher, who may often, however, delegate this authority partly or entirely to his executive editor or chief editorial writer.

Sometimes the editorials call for action. The *Hutchinson* (Kansas) *News* conducted a four-year, relentless editorial campaign that finally won democratic reapportionment of the state's legislative districts. And J. Oliver Emmerich, editor of the *McComb* (Mississippi) *Enterprise-Journal,* campaigned for civil rights though a cross was burned on his lawn, his paper was fired upon, and a Molotov cocktail was tossed into his managing editor's home.

Many, if not most, papers run only one editorial daily. It is usually written by the managing editor or one of his assistants, occasionally by the Washington correspondent or a top reporter; perhaps by the publisher himself.

Some papers find that one person can both write the daily editorial and edit the page, which includes letters to the editor, signed columns of commentators, and other editorial features. But the biggest papers have staffs of editorial writers, up to half a dozen. The leading editorial is done by the chief (or editor of the editorial page, as he is also sometimes called), who also assigns the others to his staff.

"What if an editorial writer is ordered to express an opinion he disagrees with?" Adolph S. Ochs, founder of the modern *New York Times,* was asked once. "But that has never happened!" Mr. Ochs replied.

Only men with views acceptable to the publisher are engaged as editorial writers. If a disagreement should come up, the writer could decline the assignment; if it happened often, he would have to find a publisher he agreed with.

As you might expect, editorial writers are journalists with long experience and the confidence of the publisher, and therefore usually middle-aged, even elderly, men. However, it is becoming the modern fashion to pick a young man to be editor of the editorial page when a crusader is wanted.

The Cowles newspaper chain made John R. Harrison publisher of its *Gainesville* (Florida) *Daily Sun* when he was only twenty-eight. He began writing forceful editorials, which three years later won him a Pultizer Prize for influencing reform of the city housing code.

Chapter Nine

WHAT NEWSPAPERMEN DO
—THE EDITORS

Copyreaders, or copyeditors as they are also called, are the men and women who edit reporters' copy and write headlines. They are the most numerous group of editors on a newspaper, up to one-fifth as large as the reporting staff.

Their editing job is critical rather than creative, intended to improve copy without rewriting it. They correct errors of fact and syntax, make terms conform to the paper's style, cut to space orders. They must know what information each story should contain and be sensitive to good writing. Above all, they must be preoccupied with accuracy. Since they may have to edit ten to twenty columns in seven hours on a limitless variety of subjects, they cannot check everything. They therefore memorize a huge store of miscellaneous data, try to turn themselves into living *Information Please Almanacs*.

There is a traditional feud between writers and copyreaders. The former charge the latter are frustrated authors who vent their jealousy by spoiling the stories of others. Copyreaders retort it is they, anonymous and unappreciated, who are responsible for many a writer's reputation.

John J. Corry, who has been both a reporter and a copyreader, told in Harvard's "Nieman Reports" of a new woman reporter who was unable to write her story of the Easter Parade and retired to the ladies' room in tears. A kindly old copyreader wrote the story for her and put her by-line on it. The story won a bonus from the publisher. The girl reporter hasn't spoken to the kindly old copy-reader since!

Ideally, the copyreader enters into a partnership with the writer, and both share responsibility for the story.

Writing headlines is the copyreader's task alone. It is a neat trick. Heads must epitomize the news, each line properly phrased, yet counted letter by letter to fit the column width. It takes long training to do it well and fast. Some copyreaders are experts in bright heads like these:

INAUGURAL ROBOTS INVITE MANY
INVITE MANY TWICE

PULLED IS SWITCH WRONG,
REVERSE INTO GOES CITY

Copyreaders sit together at a big, arc-shaped desk. Each man is equipped with soft, black (never blue) pencils, shears, pastepot,

COPYREADERS: They edit stories written by reporters and write headlines. Their tools are soft black pencil, spike and pastepot. (*The New York Times*)

and a "deadhook" (spike) for discarded matter. The head of the desk sits in the "slot," or center of the inner edge. The "slotman" indicates the size of head and length of story he wants on each article, and deals it out to his copyreaders on the "rim." The edited story and headline comes back to him for approval before it is sent to the composing room.

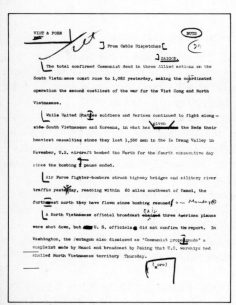

EDITED COPY: An example of a news story after editing on the copydesk. "Forn" indicates the story is to be edited by the foreign copydesk. The inscription, "Nuts," means the copy is to be set indented one en from each margin. The blue lines are put on by the printer after the copy is set. (*New York Herald Tribune*)

Most newspapers have one large "universal" copydesk to handle all copy for the paper. Some large papers have separate local, national, and foreign copydesks. Papers with large sub-departments may also have small specialized copydesks for sports, women's news, and so forth. A big Washington bureau will have its own copydesk, too. Even on a universal copydesk, however, the tendency is for copyreaders to become more or less specialized.

Only the slotman is expected to know everything about everything.

The job of copyreader may be a first step toward an important post as editor. The line of promotion is from the rim to the slot, to assistant editor, to editor of the city, national, or foreign staff, or even to managing editor.

Formerly, copyreaders were always ex-reporters, but the modern practice is to accept some beginners (though rarely women) on the desk.

CITY (METROPOLITAN) EDITOR

Next to the managing editor, the city editor is the most important editor in the shop. He is responsible for covering news of the local area, which means the bulk of all news for the paper, and he directs the local reporters, largest group on the staff.

How does the city editor decide what to cover? Some news tips are obvious—the wire service assignment schedule for the day, news coming in on the teletype, follows on yesterday's stories, tips from press agents. However, it is by originating ideas for stories that the city editor proves his mettle.

Every New York City paper carried the news story of a woman stabbed to death on a residential street one March night in 1964. But only Abe Rosenthal, *The New York Times* metropolitan editor, had the imagination to follow it up by sending a reporter to ask the thirty-eight neighbors who heard her screams for help why they did not call the police.

A big local story, such as the transit strike in New York City, puts a city editor to a supreme test. He must immediately visualize all the many separate angles and stories within the situation and assign reporters to cover and coordinate them.

To do that efficiently, he must know not only his city and his job, but also the talents and weaknesses of his men.

Fitting the right reporter to a story, bringing out the best in each one, hiring youngsters who will develop well—all that is an art that rests on intuition. Either an editor has it or he doesn't.

In the old Park Row days, the cliché for city editor was an old curmudgeon who drove reporters like galley slaves and fired them on Christmas Eve. In recent years, young city editors have come into fashion. Some are in their twenties and anyone over forty is likely to be considered too ancient for appointment. And no editor abuses reporters today; good reporters are too scarce.

City editors are usually selected from among the best local reporters or rewritemen or heads of copydesks. A usual, though

CITY EDITOR: He commands from middle of big, open city room, overseeing staff of local reporters. (*The New York Times*)

not invariable, line of promotion from city editor is to assistant managing editor and managing editor.

On an afternoon paper, the city editor will be in charge from about 8:00 A.M. to 4:00 P.M., when the bulk of the news is breaking, and when the editions go to press. On a morning paper, he will be in charge for the eight hours before the first edition closes, say from 1:00 to 9:00 P.M.

ASSISTANT CITY EDITORS

An assistant city editor makes the assignments before the city editor comes on. Large reportorial staffs may have several assistants, one of whom supervises coverage of suburban news, another statewide news, a third perhaps cultural news.

On morning papers, an assistant called night city editor comes on duty a few hours before the city editor goes home and remains in charge afterward. His main duty is to give reporters' stories a preliminary reading before passing them on to the copydesk. He also makes assignments to late-breaking stories.

Being an assistant city editor is not a guarantee of becoming city editor.

FOREIGN EDITOR

Chosen from the most experienced correspondents, the foreign editor, based at home, makes assignments to the staff abroad. He also is expected to originate ideas for news and feature stories, since there is no use in duplicating the work of the wire services. He ranks a little higher than the chief foreign correspondent.

On big staffs, he also has an assistant who makes routine assignments and takes over in his absence.

NATIONAL EDITOR

Since the national desk receives news from Washington as well as the rest of the country, an enormous flood of copy pours over it every day. The national editor makes Washington assignments through the chief of the bureau, who details his correspondents to each story. The editor makes assignments to other domestic correspondents directly. If he needs a reporter where he has none, he borrows one from the city editor.

On national disasters, the national editor takes over. Seven hours after President Kennedy was assassinated in Dallas, *The New York Times* went to press with fifty stories contributed by eighty of its reporters throughout the world, filling the first sixteen pages of the paper. Seven extra copyreaders were borrowed to augment the national copydesk that day.

MANAGING EDITOR AND ASSISTANTS

The managing editor is the boss of the newsroom. He has come up through the ranks, been a top reporter, a Washington correspondent, a city editor or assistant managing editor. In addition to supervising the entire editorial operation, he has administrative duties, the final word in hiring and firing, granting pay raises and expenses.

He represents the publisher in negotiations with labor unions, at meetings of newspaper managements, and in public relations. Some papers have also an executive editor, who is simply a super-managing editor.

The boss has assistant managing editors, who supervise news personnel, plant and equipment, travel and communications, news development and plan coverage of big events, like national political conventions, for him.

The assistant who makes the final check of news, pictures and headlines is the news editor. He also is in charge of putting the news into the paper, deciding what stories will go on Page One, laying it out in diagram, and designing other display pages as well.

His orders are carried out and the rest of the paper diagrammed, page by page, by makeup men who, as lockup time nears, oversee the work of printers in the composing room.

The news editor and his assistants have come up from the ranks of copyreaders.

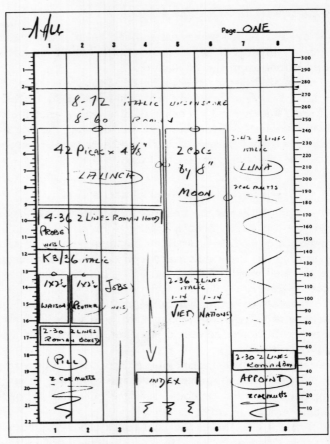

MAKEUP DIAGRAM: Makeup editor's diagram of Page One, indicating placing of stories identified by slugs, "Luna," "Launch," "Moon," "Viet," etc.; the column width and length of each story size, and kind of type of each headline: "2-col. Mutts" means the copy is to be set two columns wide, indented one-em from each margin. (*New York Herald Tribune*)

Opposite Page: **COMPLETED PAGE:** Here is a proof of the finished page after setting in type from the makeup diagram. (*New York Herald Tribune*)

WEATHER
Today: Partly cloudy and fair.
Tomorrow: Fair and cold.
TEMPERATURE RANGE
Yesterday: 37-39. Today: 27-34.
HUMIDITY
Yesterday: 3 p. m. 74%. Today: 45%.
Reports and Maps—Page 20

NEW YORK
Herald Tribune

THE LATE CITY

Established 125 Years Ago. A European Edition Is Published Daily in Paris

VOL. CXXV No. 43,404 | 230 West 41st Street, New York, N. Y. 10036 Telephone PEnnsylvania 6-4000 | FRIDAY, FEBRUARY 4, 1966 | TEN CENTS

On the Moon Softly

Russians Land First Lunar Laboratory

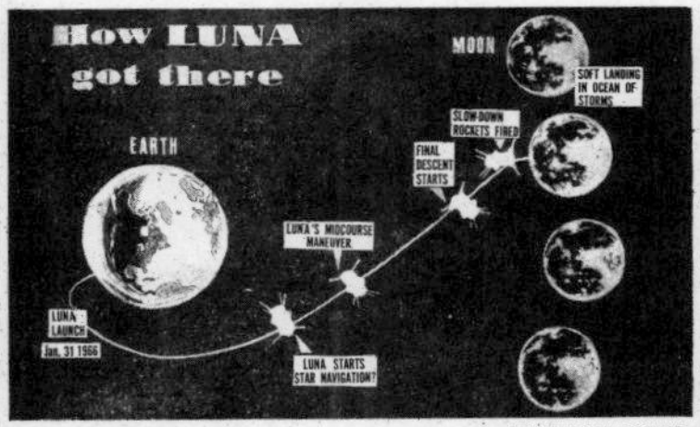

Herald Tribune chart by SAL CONTRERA

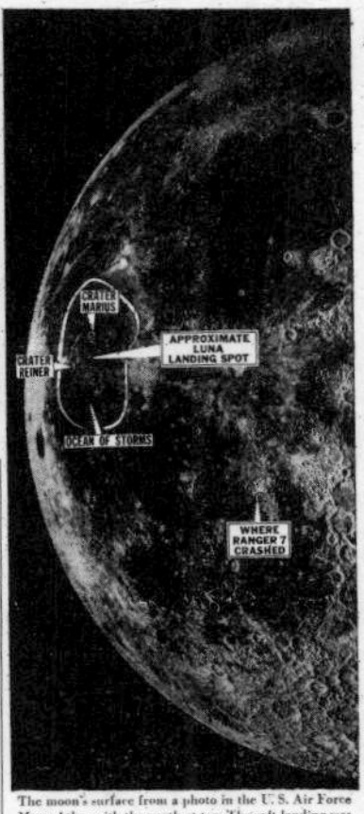

The moon's surface from a photo in the U. S. Air Force Moon Atlas, with the north at top. The soft landing was made west of the two craters in the Ocean of Storms.

Radio Signals: Yes, Man Can Walk Surface

By Earl Ubell
Science Editor

The Soviet Union stepped forth into the hot dawn of the moon yesterday by softly setting down a foot and a voice. The foot, made of cool metal, touched the forlorn surface at 1:45 p.m. EST. The voice, a radio, chirped back across 224,000 miles of void: All is well.

With nothing more than that, man's first soft lunar landing has already spoken volumes about the earth's natural satellite: for one thing, the surface is hard enough to sustain the weight of a ship of more than 3,000 pounds. Some scientists feared a sea of dust would engulf the first packet of instruments.

Thus did Luna 9, launched Monday from the Soviet Union, make history for Soviet science and for the world. It confirmed that men could one day walk on the barren lunar surface and that radio signals could be sent from a landed ship.

Momentarily, the Soviet scientists may announce that they also have an eye, a television camera taking ultra-close pictures on the ground. The giant radio telescope at Jodrell Bank, England, picked up a bagpipe skirl of radio signals they said indicated a flow of pictures.

TV or not, the landing of Luna 9 places the Soviet Union ahead in one phase of the race to the moon. In May, the scientists at Jet Propulsion Laboratory will launch a first soft-landing Surveyor from Cape Kennedy.

As one JPL man said yesterday: "Now I know how it feels to be Avis."

However, the long haul in getting a man to the moon has the character of a steeplechase: one stumble at a barrier and the race is lost. And there are many technical obstacles to be hurdled before a man arrives there.

President Johnson promptly congratulated the Soviets on their achievement in a telegram to Soviet President Nikolai V. Podgorny. Mr. Johnson called it a "major contribution to man's knowledge of the moon and of space."

EARLIER ATTEMPTS

As usual, the Russians played the game very cagily, limiting themselves to a brief announcement from Tass in Moscow:

"Today, on Feb. 3, 1966, at 21:45 Moscow time (1:45 p. m. EST), the automatic station Luna 9, launched Jan. 31, has made a soft landing on the surface of the moon in the area of the Ocean of Storms to the west of the craters Reiner and Marius.

"Radio contact with the station on the surface of the moon is reliable. Transmissions are on 183.538 megacycles. The instruments on board the station are functioning normally."

The Ocean of Storms, on the extreme eastern edge of the moon, is a relatively smooth area. It might well be a landing spot for future astronauts. Because the Russians did not give exact co-ordinates of the site, it is difficult to locate Luna 9 exactly. It is standing probably on the edge of dawn and will be in daylight for nearly two weeks as the sun creeps over the surface. Daytime temperature on the moon is 250 degrees Fahrenheit.

Lacking any specific information about Luna 9, one can only say that it probably has the following elements: one or more radio antennas which can direct signals back to earth; a landing gear to take up the shock of touch-down; a slowing rocket to cut the speed back from 6,000 miles an hour; a celestial navigation system, probably using the stars as beacons; and some sort of radar for the close approach.

Four earlier attempts by the Soviet Union ended in failure. Once they did not make a proper mid-course correction with an on-board rocket and missed the moon.

More on SOFT LANDING—P 6

Jones: Housing Charge Malicious; Robinson: Powell, Jones Territory

By Martin J. Steadman
Of The Herald Tribune Staff

Tammany Hall leader J. Raymond Jones yesterday denied that he ever told a member of the Housing and Redevelopment Board that there was a lot of money to be made in housing "for anyone—in or out of office."

The Tammany chieftain told the State Commission of Investigation that the man who made the accusation the day before, Earl Brown, was "malicious and vindictive."

In the sixth day of public hearings into charges of waste, inefficiency, profiteering and political influence in the city's $1.5 billion middle-income housing program, the SCI also heard former baseball star Jackie Robinson testify that he lost out as a sponsor of a Harlem apartment house project because it was "reserved for Rep. Adam Clayton) Powell and Jones."

Another political name dropped into the hearings was Bronx Democratic Rep. James Scheuer, who is a nationally known builder. Mr. Jones testified that an attempt was made to get the housing project for Mr. Scheuer. The application came before Mr. Scheuer was elected as a Reform candidate in 1964, and no suggestion of impropriety was imputed to him. Mr. Scheuer said in Washington he didn't recall talking to Mr. Jones.

The project, a $40 million venture known as Esplanade Gardens, was approved last September by the HRB. Its sponsors include the wife of a captain in Mr. Jones' political club, and Daniel Burrows, a business partner of the Tammany leader.

The statement by Mr. Robinson was the first indication that Rep. Powell may have had a personal interest in the project.

The Congressman has been invited to testify by the SCI, but so far there has been no word from Washington on whether he will take the stand.

On Wednesday, Mr. Brown had offered a variety of quotes he attributed to Mr. Jones in a conversation they had about Esplanade Gardens in January or February of 1962.

Mr. Brown, who is now the executive director of the Commission on Human Rights, told the SCI that Mr. Jones told him:

"Any member of the board who supports this project ought never to want for money again."

Yesterday, Mr. Jones not only emphatically denied saying that to Mr. Brown, he swore that Mr. Brown had come to him "to beg me to help a friend of his get the project."

Asked by Commissioner Goodman Sarachan who that friend was, Mr. Jones, a Democrat, testified that it was Mr. Scheuer, who was not in office at that time.

"I spoke with Mr. Scheuer, who is a developer of inte-

More on JONES—P 3

Commission Calls for Federal Subsidy

Guaranteed Income for All

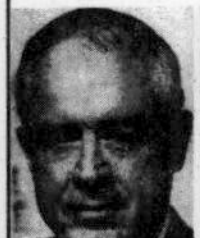

Thomas J. Watson jr.

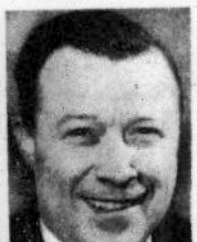

Walter Reuther

By Douglas Kiker
Of The Herald Tribune Staff

WASHINGTON.

The Federal government should guarantee every American family a minimum annual income and should also institute a vast, new public "service" program which would place the nation's chronically unemployed on U.S. payrolls.

Those two recommendations are among those made by a Presidential blue-ribbon National Commission on Technology, Automation and Economic Progress. The committee's sweeping, controversial report was released by the White House yesterday.

Under the proposed minimum income plan, the Federal government would make up the difference between a family's annual income and an established minimum standard.

COST

It could cost from $2 billion to $20 billion a year, depending on its scope, and as many as 35 million people could be affected by it if a minimum income were set at $3,000 a year.

The 14-member commission was established by Congress in 1964. Its members, appointed by the President, include labor, business, economic, civic and government leaders, who have been meeting two days a month for the last year and a half, in an attempt to find long-range national solutions for the growing problem of a growing population faced with increasing "technological unemployment."

Almost every recommendation contained in their detailed, 210-page report was unanimous. All of them are ambitious. Many of them are bound to be controversial. The White House said yesterday

More on MINIMUM—P 6

Dogs Malignant—Halt Pill Tests on Women

By David Hoffman
Of The Herald Tribune Staff

WASHINGTON.

A group of 340 women have taken an experimental birth control pill that laboratory tests indicate may cause breast cancer in dogs, the Food and Drug Administration reported yesterday.

Merck, Sharpe & Dohme, the pill's manufacturer, halted all human and animal tests immediately after finding microscopic cancers in the breasts of two test dogs, the FDA said.

The canine cancers were discovered before the new oral contraceptive was approved by the government for prescription sale. Thus far, no trace of cancer has appeared among the women given the drug in closely supervised clinical trials, but the FDA said they will receive long-term exams under a Merck program.

Dr. James Goddard, the FDA's newly appointed commissioner, denied yesterday there was any evidence that oral contraceptives now on the market could cause cancer, even in dogs. But, he added, "You're always concerned when you find this kind of effect" in the laboratory.

Called MK-665 by Merck, the drug is a blend of Mestranol, an estrogen commonly used in oral contraceptives now on the market, and ethynerone, a progestational agent synthesized by the company. Asked why ethynerone

More on BIRTH PILL—P 19

U. S. Won't Press UN on Viet Issue

FIGHTING

From Cable Dispatches

SAIGON.

The total confirmed Communist dead in three Allied actions on the South Vietnamese coast rose to 1,082 yesterday.

It made the co-ordinated operation the second costliest of the war for the Viet Cong and North Vietnamese.

While United States soldiers and Marines continued to fight alongside South Vietnamese and Koreans, in what has given the Reds their heaviest casualties since they lost 1,500 men in the Ia Drang Valley in November, U. S. aircraft bombed the North for the fourth consecutive day since the bombing pause ended.

Air Force fighter-bombers struck highway bridges and military river traffic yesterday, reaching within 60 miles southwest of Hanoi, the fur-

More on ALLIED—P 5

TALKING

By Darius S. Jhabvala
Of The Herald Tribune Staff

UNITED NATIONS.

The United States will not press for a formal discussion or for the adoption of a resolution by the UN Security Council on the crisis in Viet Nam, a reliable source said yesterday.

The U. S. draft resolution circulated to all members on Monday, which almost surely would have been vetoed by the Soviet delegation, is now intended merely as guidelines for private negotiations.

CONTRAST

According to the source, the objective of the U. S. in bringing the Viet Nam issue before the Council was "to stimulate further peace moves." The decision was made in the wake of North Viet Nam's refusal to respond favorably to American peace initiatives.

The source pointed out that U. S. officials expected the dramatic two-day Council session to trigger discussions and reconsiderations of positions in the world's capitals.

To the present position of not pressing for Council discussion and resolution, is in apparent contrast with the U. S. position of last Monday, when Ambassador Arthur Goldberg requested "an urgent meeting of the Council," and appealed to that body to address "itself urgently and positively . . . and exert its most rigorous endeavors and its immense prestige to finding a

More on UN—P 5

IN THE NEWS THIS MORNING

Lindsay Judge List: Rosenberg and Mollen

By Paul Weissman
Of The Herald Tribune Staff

Mayor Lindsay has proposed Gustave Rosenberg, chairman of the Board of Higher Education, for a Criminal Court judgeship it was learned yesterday.

The name of Milton Mollen, Mr. Lindsay's unsuccessful running mate for Controller, was also among those given to the Mayor's Committee on the Judiciary as a candidate to fill six vacant Criminal Court positions. Appointments to the $25,000-a-year posts are for 10 years.

Other names sent to Louis M. Loeb, chairman of the 15-member committee include:

- Joseph A. Macchia, manager of Mr. Lindsay's 1958 primary campaign, for U. S. Representative.
- Daniel Hoffman, former president of the Marshal's Association of the City of New York and a Brooklyn borough coordinator in Lindsay's mayoralty campaign.
- Eugene Canudo, a former Magistrate who ran unsuccessfully with Rudolph Halley on the Liberal party ticket in 1933 for President of the City Council when his term expired and once served as a secretary to the late Mayor Fiorello La Guardia.
- Donald Jacoby, a former law assistant in Kings County Supreme Court who was appointed to a 26-hour term as a Criminal Court judge by Mayor Wagner.

The committee is considering these and other names for the posts. A seventh vacancy, for a Family Court judge-

More on LINDSAY—P 6

Chapter Ten

WHAT NEWSPAPERMEN DO
—PICTURE MEN

Newspapers—influenced by television and picture magazines—devote more of their space to news pictures today than ever before. Leading stories are illustrated by a photograph, and editors make an effort to print at least one picture on every page.

Many of these photographs come on contract from the wire services (by teleprinting machines that transmit clear photos by wire and radio from all over the world with incredible speed). Other photographs are offered free by press agents and other news sources.

Every newspaper also takes some photographs of its own—though the majority do not employ a full-time photographer. The bigger papers will employ one; the largest, particularly in New York, a dozen or more photographers.

Outside of cities like New York and Washington, it is more and more common for reporters to snap their own pictures. Correspondents for even the biggest papers frequently carry a camera as well as a portable typewriter. Skill as a photographer is rarely required of a reporter, and no one expects him to create art like Ansel Adams. Generally it is enough to be able to bring back clear, sharp shots; if a cub reporter does not know how to use a camera, the city editor will assign someone to show him.

A few papers, however, have gone further.

"We have trained all our bureau chiefs and reporters to use cameras," Billy Davis, director of photography of the *Louisville*

Courier-Journal and Times, reported in *Editor and Publisher* recently. "They're not trained just to pull the camera release, but to compose and light a pleasing picture. This is a trend, whether we as professional photographers like it or not."

To take advantage of the trend, you may take photo-journalism courses in journalism school, or practice taking pictures on your own.

NEWS PHOTOGRAPHERS

Full-time newspaper photographers rarely come from journalism school; or indeed from the colleges. Editors do not care whether their photographers have had any education at all, as long as they bring back exclusive pictures that tell the story, shots that, as the *New York Daily News* says, "hit you like a punch in the nose."

To make a reputation, a photographer should have a sharp eye for the telling detail, as well as a recognition of the dramatic moment.

William E. Gallagher of the *Flint* (Mich.) *Journal* won national recognition by getting a shot of the late Adlai Stevenson campaigning for the Presidency with a hole in his shoe. William C. Beall of the *Washington* (D.C.) *Daily News* won a Pulitzer Prize, not for an important news shot, but for the photograph of a policeman reasoning with a two-year-old boy trying to get closer to a parade.

You can get a start as a photographer by taking pictures on your own of accidents, parades, fires, riots, and so on, and peddling them to editors. Or you may begin as an employe of an agency that makes pictures of accidents for insurance companies or of industrial processes and plants for commercial companies.

You may also break in as "lab boy," developing and printing photographs in a newspaper's darkroom. You will have a chance to learn from veteran photographers on the staff, and if you show promise you will get a chance to go out with a camera as an apprentice on a news story.

All newspaper staff photographers are general assignment men, covering all kinds of news events and features. Some of the biggest papers station a photographer in Washington, another at a

"JUST ONE MORE, MR. PRESIDENT!" Photographers,
too, cover White House for all media.

place in the news like Vietnam, and perhaps another on roving
duty in Europe.

PICTURE EDITOR

Papers that use many photographs daily employ a picture editor
to assign photographers, pick pictures to be printed, order their
size, and write the captions. Smaller papers put all these duties
onto the city editor or his assistant, except caption writing, which

is done on the copydesk. The picture editor may be a former photographer or a copyreader with experience in picking pictures.

ARTISTS

Editorial cartoonists are a rare and beautiful species that is dying out, although a few old-timers, like Herb Block, survive. Some cartoonists remain on sports pages, and a very few artists are retained to make sketches in law courts and other places from which cameras are barred. Newspaper artists today are usually reduced to drawing maps and diagrams and to retouching photos.

Chapter Eleven

YOUR CHANCES
ON NEWSPAPERS

Newspapers are still the most important medium of journalism. Day in, day out they remain our main supply of news, particularly local news. They are also the largest employer of journalists.

Newspaper work is still the basis of all journalistic skills. A competent newspaperman can learn rather quickly to adapt to other media, but it rarely happens that a journalist gets his start on magazines or broadcasting and then moves to a newspaper.

Yet, these other fields of journalism are cutting deeply into the supply of young journalists. Only 17 percent of 1965 journalism graduates went into daily newspapers, as against 40 percent ten years earlier. They now fill only one out of seven of the available openings.

However, the findings of Alvin E. Austin, chairman of journalism at North Dakota University, must be considered: "Newspapers of outstanding quality seldom have any shortage of applicants."

THE BEST NEWSPAPERS

The best newspapers are published in the largest cities. But 1,000 of the dailies are put out in towns of under 25,000 population. Of the remaining 750, only 200 are rated as "major" and only 18 of these "first rate" by Dean Edward Barrett of the Columbia University Graduate School of Journalism.

Which are they?

A survey of journalism teachers' opinion by John Tebbel for the

Saturday Review gave this list: *The New York Times, Christian Science Monitor, Wall Street Journal, St. Louis Post-Dispatch, Milwaukee Journal, Washington Post, New York Herald Tribune, Louisville Courier-Journal, Chicago Tribune, Chicago Daily News, Baltimore Sun, Atlanta Constitution, Minneapolis Tribune, Kansas City Star, Los Angeles Times,* in that order.

A survey of publishers' opinion by Edward L. Bernays, public relations expert, resulted in the same list, with the *Detroit Press* and *Miami Herald* inserted about midway.

A survey of editors' opinion by *Scholastic Magazine* added the *Des Moines Register* about halfway down.

By and large, these eighteen are the best newspapers to work for in terms of wages, working conditions, prestige and professional satisfaction—and the hardest on which to get jobs. Available jobs on other papers should not be scorned.

MIDDLE- AND SMALLER-SIZE PAPERS

"It seems to me obvious that success can come more quickly to a talented young journalist on a middle-sized paper," says Charles T. Alexander, Jr., who himself left *The Washington* (D.C.) *Evening Star* to become managing editor of the much smaller *Wilmington* (Del.) *Morning News and Evening Journal.* "He gets the opportunity to tackle big assignments sooner, to acquire more varied experience—and to gain professional satisfaction at an earlier stage.

"On a smaller paper, a good city editor can give his staff of ten to fifteen reporters individual supervision and training. Those reporters will have generally started at a pay scale commensurate with or even slightly above that of the larger dailies. They can become specialists—or, over the years, expert in many facets of their craft."

Mr. Alexander adds that medium-size cities are good places in which to live and challenging places in which to work.

WHAT EDITORS SAY

Here is a sampling of what editors of some leading newspapers say about their job opportunities for beginners:

Norman E. Isaacs, executive editor, *Louisville* (Ky.) *Courier-Journal and the Louisville Times:* "We've been averaging four a year fresh out of graduate schools. . . . Personal traits? . . . intelligence, character, honesty and a passion to be a newspaperman. . . . If they're good, they can move up very rapidly."

Clayton Kirkpatrick, managing editor, *Chicago Tribune:* "We've been hiring from twelve to twenty reporters and copyreaders each year. Approximately one-half of these are beginners from university campuses, with no more than part-time experience. We prefer recruits with a bachelor's or a master's degree. The majority have their degree in journalism, but we do not insist on this. We look for candidates who have demonstrated they can write, usually on their college papers, and for evidence of desire for a journalistic career. Usually this is demonstrated by an early and continuing interest through high school and university. We like to see a record of outstanding scholastic achievement."

Cruise Palmer, managing editor, *The Kansas City Star:* "Each summer we bring in about ten college journalism students, mostly pre-seniors, to take up the vacation slack on our staffs. From this group a year or two later we select most of our starting reporters. Getting five or six good men and women a year is not a problem. We prefer new staff members with journalism degrees because they have more savvy . . . but we don't rule out good English or political science majors who demonstrate real desire to get into journalism. We rate enthusiasm for newspaper work high. We bring staffers along according to aptitude as fast as they are able to move. All jobs from assistant city editor up are always filled from staff."

Arthur R. Bertelson, managing editor, *St. Louis Post-Dispatch:* "Under an interne arrangement with the University of Michigan, we take on every summer a graduate of journalism school or one doing graduate work in journalism. In the ten years that this system has been operating, we have added six or seven first-class workmen to our staff. In addition, the Newspaper Guild here awards a fellowship (summer employment at the *Post-Dispatch*), and this has supplied us with two outstanding people. . . . We don't require journalism graduates. . . . We look for some writing talent and like to have our people major in English, history, political science. . . . I look mostly for dedication to journalism as a profession, outgoing personality, evidence of aggressiveness and intellectual curiosity. . . . I have had more than 100 young people write since the first of the year wanting jobs. . . ."

William I. Ray, Jr., executive editor, *The Atlanta Journal* and *The Atlanta Constitution:* "We average openings for five beginners a year on each of our newspapers. . . . We seek beginners who want to write . . . usually journalism school graduates, although some are liberal arts graduates with demonstrated writing desires, such as college newspaper work. . . . The industry does have a shortage of qualified beginners . . . we do not . . . since we are a major newspaper with good working conditions."

David Starr, executive editor, *Long Island* (N.Y.) *Press:* "We take two beginners a year, picked usually from two or three summer internes and colleges students working summers as copyboys. I want a beginner to have a liberal arts education, majoring in history, political economy, government or economics. I approve of journalism school as a one-year, graduate course only. I make no particular demand for specialized knowledge or brilliant writing ability. The highest recommendation a boy can bring me is that he has worked on his high school and college paper for four years, and summers on a newspaper. . . . We look for aggressiveness in going after a story, resourcefulness, alertness, accuracy, sober judgment and a wide background of miscellaneous information. . . . All applicants get a one day's tryout as a reporter. . . ."

Some leading papers will not take beginners. Murray M. Weiss, former managing editor of the *New York Herald Tribune,* says the "Guild contract makes training a reporter expensive indeed." Turner Catledge, executive editor of *The New York Times,* says, "What we want are twenty-five-year-olds with forty years of experience."

Abraham M. Rosenthal, *The Times* metropolitan editor, advises beginners to work for four or five years on big city papers in the South, "where the action is," and to produce not only news but also magazine articles and books on a wide variety of subjects.

"We demand a good general education, superior intelligence, broad interest in life, and, above all, superior writing skill," he says. "We are the best paper in the world, we pay the highest salaries, and therefore demand the best reporters. Everybody we hire is on a five months' trial."

A WOMAN'S CHANCES

Discrimination against women has always existed in newspapers. About 80 percent of all employes on newspapers are male. However, women are gaining now; about one-third of all beginners' jobs on newspapers are currently being filled by girls.

"The newspaper business is a man's business," says Marjorie Paxson, national president of Theta Sigma Phi, women's journalistic sorority, and assistant women's editor of the *Miami Herald.* "It's a man's world . . . tough, highly competitive, and no woman, no matter how deserving, is likely to get a promotion if there's a man around who can do the job."

The real reason editors are reluctant to hire and train women, Miss Paxson believes, is that "they never know when the girls will get married and pregnant and leave. And it's a valid objection."

Editors seldom admit that, however. Their most frequently stated objection is that much of the work is too perilous or arduous for a woman.

"Editors still have reluctance to take women on general assignment or work that could lead them at night into dangerous territory," says Michael J. Ogden, managing editor of the *Providence* (R.I.) *Journal and Evening Bulletin.*

Murray Weiss says: "We frown on women as district reporters, covering stories that require relatively great physical exertion and often some degree of danger."

"They can't for the most part cover murders, rapes, robberies and crimes of violence," adds Arthur Bertelson of the *St. Louis Post-Dispatch.* "And they are usually disinterested in politics and governmental affairs. I have yet to encounter a woman as versatile as a man in the reporting business. Of course, this may be our fault for not experimenting more with women and perhaps that will be changed in the future."

Clayton Kirkpatrick of the *Chicago Tribune* says he has many women on his staff but "we do not choose to send women on the streets on assignment at night."

Women charge this attitude is unjustified. They insist upon the right to accept danger and discomfort like a man. They proudly point to famous war correspondents like Dickey Chapelle, who covered eight wars in eight years, and Marguerite Higgins, who covered fighting in World War II, Korea and Vietnam. They complain that there is even a ban against women in many jobs that are not at all dangerous or physically hard. And the refusal to make a capable woman boss over men is simply, as Murray Weiss admits, that the "male mentality is living in a different era."

Despite discrimination, some authorities like Herbert Brucker, editor of the *Hartford Courant* and past president of the American Society of Newspaper Editors, believe there is no limit to the kind of assignments a capable woman can get on newspapers now.

And it is a fact that at least one woman has broken into every kind of newspaper job, even police and criminal court reporting. So many women have turned up to cover sports events that two major football conferences had to admit them to the press box, long restricted to men. Women have become top feature writers and columnists on some papers.

Foreign Assignments   Women are occasionally sent out on foreign assignments, but few on a permanent basis, and then sometimes only because they are married to foreign correspondents. Among notable women correspondents were Flora Lewis, who served in London and Warsaw for the *Washington Post,* and Ruby Hart Phillips in Havana for *The New York Times*.

Women in Washington   Women have excellent opportunities as Washington correspondents, though, as usual, not so good as men.

No women are yet admitted to either of the Congressional press galleries (nor, incidentally, as members of the Washingon Press Club). Many women reporters are relegated to the women's angle of the news—for example, covering the President's wife, children and household, but not the President himself. They also get sweet features like the cherry blossom festival and human interest stories of tourists.

Nevertheless, many women have proved their competence as reporters of virtually all kinds of government news. Sarah McClendon has occasionally outdone the sharpest men in quizzing the President at press conferences. Eileen Shanahan is strictly an economics and financial expert. Doris Fleeson has turned out a syndicated column on Washington politics for many years.

When Ruth Finney retired recently as Washington correspondent for Scripps-Howard papers, her editor-in-chief, Walker Stone, said: "In forty-two years, we never asked her to do a woman's angle on a story. She was far too proficient in too many other things."

Women Deskmen and Editors Traditionally, women have been barred from the newspaper copydesk. This is strange because there is always a scarcity of good copyreaders and women have proved to be capable editors on magazines. There is nothing about the work that makes it unsuitable for a woman. Yet, few newspapers will hire any.

Betsy Wade, first of three women to be seated on the rim at *The New York Times,* recalls that at first she was treated by her male colleagues as an amusing mascot, a freak they hoped would go away.

But Betsy stayed. "The desk is a good place for a woman to work," she says. "And what could be nicer than being surrounded by men?"

Women are nearly always passed over in choosing a city editor, on the ground that men reporters will not gladly take orders from them. But in the rare cases where a woman has been tried, the experiment has been successful. For example, Mrs. K. C. Kuhns has been city editor of the *Kokomo* (Indiana) *Tribune* since 1961 with no revolt by her predominantly male staff.

"I may have to use more diplomacy than a man," "Casey" says, "but I can stand and slug it out when I have to."

Her only problem is that visitors mistake her for the city editor's secretary.

A Woman's Best Chances For a few newspaper jobs, a woman is preferred. A "woman's touch" is called for on many feature stories, a fact that has helped some women to become top feature writers and columnists. Women are wanted to cover social welfare news, and they are often chosen as editors of education or religion, and as critics of the arts.

A girl's best chances of employment are in women's departments, covering the traditional specialties—society, food, fashion, homemaking, child raising. Talented, ambitious girls resent this and often turn down such jobs.

"That is a serious error," Norman Isaacs argues. "These departments are changing all over the country. They're becoming news departments with focus on family interests. When Mrs. Lyndon Johnson visited here, our women's department took over coverage. Girls have a chance to crack the barrier through women's departments, but they have a negative reaction. They're building their own job limitations."

There are numerous examples to illustrate Mr. Isaacs' argument.

Nan Robertson, whose stories from Washington frequently hit the front page of *The New York Times,* made her reputation with bright feature stories on *The Times* woman's pages.

Ruth Seltzer of the *Philadelphia Bulletin* has expanded her job of society editor to include coverage of horse shows, surf-casting and pheasant-shooting tournaments, tennis matches, music recitals, and art exhibitions.

Charlotte Curtis of *The New York Times,* not content to rewrite trivia sent in by mothers of brides, undertook to dissect the "in" circles of New York, Pebble Beach, Houston, and other wealthy communities. She made a reputation for keenness and wit and had a wonderful time traveling to lush resorts.

"I want to see more women in every field of news," declares

Abe Rosenthal, one of the very few editors to voice such welcome. "I think it's good for the paper."

GIRL FEATURE WRITERS: There are many on news-papers. Nan Robertson, one of the best, gets a piece about midwinter sunbathers at Coney Island. (*The New York Times*)

Chapter Twelve | **NEWSPAPER WORKING CONDITIONS AND PAY**

Working conditions in newspapers today are good, vastly better than they used to be. The newsroom of even a big daily was a dusty, decrepit place, fogged with tobacco smoke, and with spittoons for tobacco-chewers. Today, even small dailies have modern, air-conditioned buildings and steel office furniture.

For newsmen, the 5-day, 35- to 40-hour week is universal, with compensation for overtime, paid annual vacations up to four weeks, and reasonable sick leave with pay. Retirement on pension is becoming more common. There is no discharge without good cause; severance pay is usually at the rate of two weeks for every year of service.

THE A.N.G.

For these benefits, the American Newspaper Guild, organized in 1933 under the leadership of the late Heywood Broun, crusading columnist, is primarily responsible.

The A.N.G. is an American Federation of Labor—Congress of Industrial Organizations union of white collar newspaper employes, not journalists alone, but all employes in the news, advertising, promotion, circulation, and other commercial departments. On a very few papers, the Guild has also taken in some mechanical workers.

Minimum wages, hours, and working conditions of all eligible employes on 183 newspapers, 11 wire and news services, and 62 news and other magazines are governed by contract with the Guild.

Guild papers comprise only about 10 percent of all the dailies, but they represent a cross-section of them and include most of the biggest. The rest are constrained by competition to follow Guild scales more or less.

If you get a job on a Guild paper with a closed shop contract, you will be required to join the union. Many Guild papers have a "preferential" shop, meaning that a specified majority (usually 85 or 90 percent of eligible employes) must join. In practice, more than the required number of employes join voluntarily, so there is always room for a dissenter to be hired.

Nonmembers enjoy the same benefits as Guild members, but they do not pay dues or assessments. Guild dues are usually 10 percent of your weekly salary per month, and on some papers are "checked off" (withheld) from your pay.

DO NOT JUDGE BY MINIMUMS

A survey presented to the Association for Education in Journalism in 1964 found the median job income of newspapermen to be $11,300 after ten years' experience. Free-lance writing boosted their incomes in some cases to $17,000. But the sampling was small and confined to four Midwestern cities.

You cannot calculate "going" wages from Guild scales. Guild contracts set minimum wages for beginners and annual increases for three to six years. How much a newsman earns after he reaches top minimum depends upon his individual merit and the ability of the paper to pay. Some newspapers operate at Guild scale, resigned to losing good men to better paying companies when top minimums have been reached. Other papers have been forced by competition for superior men to pay above scale, even to cubs.

The *Cleveland Plain Dealer,* with 328,000 circulation, is a typical example of a newspaper which pays most of its staff members salaries above those set by contract. The highest contract minimum is $151.77; but of 187 newsmen on the staff, 123 are paid premiums from $6.87 to $126.16 a week. Thirty-six staff men earn between $200 and $250 a week, nine over $250.

On *The New York Times,* which seldom accepts a *raw* beginner into its news department, 90 percent of the newsmen earn above scale, some twice and thrice as much.

From this general information, we endorse the advice of one outstanding editor: "If you are not making above minimum after six years, it is time to resign and get a better job, in or out of the newspaper business!"

For each newspaper job, described in the preceding pages, we give below the known minimum wages and our estimate of going wages from data we have been able to obtain.

REPORTERS

The $95.74 average weekly starting pay that 1965 journalism graduates received on daily newspapers is a good indicator of what cub reporters were paid that year, since most young people start their news careers as reporters.

However, starting minimums, too, have a considerable range, depending on the size and prosperity of a paper. Here's a sampling as of 1965: the tiny *Oshawa* (N.Y.) *Times,* $50; the *St. Louis Post-Dispatch,* $100.50; *Louisville Courier-Journal and Louisville Times,* $105 for unmarried reporters, $115 for a man with wife and children; *The New York Times,* $120.25.

Raises come at the rate generally of $10 a year. Top reporter minimum on the *Oshawa Times* was $100 a week; on the *St. Louis Post-Dispatch,* $180.50; a new contract at the *Washington Post* calls for a $210 top minimum for reporters and photographers in 1968.

"Reporter" in Guild contracts includes Washington and foreign correspondents, bureau chiefs, department heads, critics, columnists, almost anyone who writes. This takes in some of the highest paid men in the business. Some top *New York Times* reporters have salaries of $500 a week.

Many reporters on the local staff also earn well above minimum, but possibly 50 percent above top minimum is about the most they can reasonably expect. Probably all specialists earn above minimum. In general they are paid more than beat men. The biggest salaries to local reporters, however, go to the top men on general assignments.

FEATURE WRITERS, CRITICS, COLUMNISTS

Most feature writers command wages above the reporters' minimum, but they will never get the highest wages unless they are also able to handle hard news. The biggest stories in any newspaper are hard-news stories, and they go to the best, highest paid reporters.

The papers that can afford full-time critics and columnists pay them like first-rank reporters, or just under the top. When a reporter is assigned to an occasional review, he is not paid anything extra: he gets a pair of free tickets, doesn't he?

The aim of every columnist is to achieve syndication, which greatly increases his income without costing his paper any more. Indeed, it makes money for his original employer. Royalty rates are set by individual bargaining; syndicated columnists may earn as little as $15,000 and as much as $250,000 a year.

REWRITEMEN

Rewritemen are paid better than the lowest rank of reporters. On many papers, there is a contract differential of $3 to $5 a week in their favor. However, rewritemen are not paid as much over the scale as top reporters. Rewritemen will earn more in general on afternoon papers than on morning papers and still more on wire services.

FOREIGN CORRESPONDENTS

Foreign correspondents are always among the highest paid reporters on the staff of the big papers; small papers cannot afford them at all. The youngest correspondent may start overseas at $200 a week. The bureau chiefs will get up to $25,000 a year. The expense account necessarily must be generous, and living allowances are paid where costs are impossibly high.

The chief correspondent will receive at least a token amount over the highest paid man on his staff.

DOMESTIC CORRESPONDENTS

All Washington correspondents are paid well above minimum for reporters. The average salary is probably not so high as foreign correspondents', because living overseas is regarded as something of a sacrifice while working in Washington is considered a privilege. Washington expense accounts are smaller, too. However, the top men in a Washington bureau will be paid as well as top foreign correspondents for the same paper.

The chief of the Washington bureau is the Number One reporter on the paper, outranking the national editor and, if it came to a showdown, anyone else below managing editor. His salary depends entirely on circumstances in each case. A chief Washington correspondent for one newspaper is said to receive $50,000 a year.

Salaries of state correspondents are commensurate with those of lower ranking Washington correspondents for the same paper.

Regional correspondents are above-minimum reporters, though not the best paid, ranking about the median salary on the staff.

Suburban reporters do not command salaries as high as any other correspondents, nor as high as the better reporters on the main office staff. Some papers put cubs on suburban beats at minimum wages. Others prefer reporters with more experience, which means slightly higher salaries.

EDITORIAL WRITERS

Editorial writers are very well paid, since most are veteran editors, correspondents, or specialist reporters, whose salary has not, of course, been cut.

COPYREADERS

Guild pay scales provide for premiums for copyreaders of up to $15 a week over reporters' minimums. Most copyreaders earn above minimum; their average pay is higher on any paper than the average of reporters. However, no copyreader, including the slotman who is, of course, the best paid on his desk, earns as much as the highest paid reporter.

CITY, NATIONAL, AND FOREIGN EDITORS

On nearly every newspaper, the city editor is more important than any other editor below assistant managing editor. He therefore is better paid than editors of other divisions, certainly more than any of his reporters.

The national editor and foreign editor will be paid like a top correspondent, but possibly not as much as the chief one, who is only nominally under their orders. In practice he is quite independent. Editors are easier to replace than writers with a popular following.

Salaries of assistants to the city, national and foreign editors are much below those of their superiors, roughly on a par with the slotman on the appropriate copy desk, sometimes less.

MANAGING EDITOR

The managing editor, by whatever title called, is the highest paid employe in the news department. Little community dailies may pay the Big Boss only $10,000 a year; some metropolitan papers in chains under a single ownership may pay him $100,000 or more, and increase his earnings further by stock dividends. But that is hardly your problem now.

Salaries of the news editor and other assistant managing editors do not approach that of the boss. But on any staff, their salaries are, obviously, comparatively high.

PHOTOGRAPHERS AND PICTURE EDITORS

The Guild minimum for photographers is the same as for reporters. However, photographers do not progress as much above minimum as reporters and nowhere near the top reporters' pay.

Picture editors are paid like a better copyreader.

FOR MORE INFORMATION

BOOKLETS, PAMPHLETS, PERIODICALS

Bulletin of American Society of Newspaper Editors. Monthly. Box 1053, Wilmington, Del.

Career as a News Correspondent. No. 269.

Career as a Newspaper Reporter. No. 174.

Career as a Sports Writer No. 266.

Career as an Editor and Careers in Editorial Work. No. 118.

News Photography as a Career. No. 202.

All available at $1 each from Careers Research Monographs, Institute for Research, 537 South Dearborn, Chicago 5, Ill.

Careers for Negroes on Newspapers. American Newspaper Guild, 1126 16th St., N.W., Washington, D.C. Free.

Careers in Newspapering. Career Information Service, New York Life Insurance Company, Box 51, Madison Square Station, New York 10, N.Y. Free.

Editor & Publisher. Weekly trade paper of newspaper industry. 850 Third Ave., New York, N.Y. 20¢

Finding a Successful Career in the Daily Newspaper Business.

How to Spot a Newsman

The American Newspaper

All available, free, from American Newspaper Publishers Association Foundation, 750 Third Avenue, New York, N.Y.

Minimum Wage Scales on More Than 180 Newspapers in U.S. and Canada. American Newspaper Guild Research Dept., 1126 16th St., N.W., Washington, D.C.

Newspaper Reporters. Occupational Outlook Bulletins: U.S. Department of Labor. Supt. of Documents, Washington 25, D.C. 5¢

The Guild Reporter. Fortnightly newspaper of American Newspaper Guild.

Editor & Publisher. Weekly trade paper of newspaper industry. 850 Third Avenue, New York, N.Y. 20¢

REFERENCE MANUALS

Ayer, N. W. *Directory of Newspapers and Periodicals.* Lists names, addresses, editors and circulation of 1,800 daily newspapers, 9,000 weekly newspapers.

Editor & Publisher Yearbook. Similar data to Ayer's.

Newspapers in this country get the great bulk of their national and foreign news from the two great wire services, The Associated Press and the United Press International. Together, they supply three-quarters of all foreign news to American newspapers and 90 percent to radio and television stations. They also distribute a huge amount of news pictures by wire.

The two wire services have been traditionally a training ground for young reporters, particularly as foreign correspondents, of whom they are by far the largest employers. While the A.P. and U.P.I. manage to hold on to some of their bright stars, many of their writers move up to top jobs on newspapers, news magazines, radio and television stations.

The Associated Press is a cooperative owned by its 1,700 member newspapers and 2,000 radio and television stations in the United States. It has also 4,000 customer papers and radio stations outside this country. It picks up news from any member and distributes it to all on the wire. It also covers some news with its own staff.

The A.P. employs 3,000 full-time persons in 125 bureaus in eighty countries. Two-thirds of these are reporters, rewritemen, copyreaders, editors, photographers. Its foreign correspondents number 268 full time, and hundreds of stringers.

The United Press International, a privately owned commercial service, has 5,800 clients (newspapers, radio and television stations) in the United States and 110 other countries. It has 10,000 employes (full-time and stringers) stationed in 62 countries, with particular concentration in Latin America. Its staff foreign correspondents total 291 plus many stringers.

The competition between the A.P. and U.P.I. is always acute, each trying to beat the other, if only by a minute or two with a news flash. The A.P. is the more conservative; the U.P.I., livelier, especially in its feature stories and columns.

THE WORK

The work of journalists on the wire services is similar to that of their opposite numbers on newspapers, the principal difference being speed. With a deadline literally every minute, the wire service reporter must keep his story moving in short "takes," perhaps one paragraph at a time. If he has no time to write that take, he telephones it to a rewriteman.

When a story is "running," that is, changing with new developments, the wire service reporter must leave the scene for a few minutes now and again to send in a take. Pat Morin of the A.P. was luckily in a street telephone booth when a mob of segregationists attacked a Little Rock, Arkansas, high school in front of him on September 23, 1957. From his glass observation booth, Morin dictated a story that won him the Pulitzer Prize.

Rewrite on a wire service can be a grinding job. On local wire services, like Chicago City News or Central Press of Cleveland, a rewriteman may have to pound out half a dozen stories almost simultaneously—first lead on each, then first add on each, second add on each, and so on, with new leads, folo new leads, inserts, corrections as necessary.

After the running story is finished, the reporter or rewriteman does a wrapup or final, complete story in one piece like an ordinary writer.

QUALIFICATIONS—U.P.I.

U.P.I. takes about fifty beginners a year into the larger of its ninety-two bureaus in this country for training.

A college degree is required; a major in political science or history, command of a foreign language, and experience on a college paper are desirable. Since the U.P.I. is strong in Latin America, Spanish and Portuguese are the tongues often demanded.

"We look first for people who like to write so much that it's almost a compulsion," says Earl J. Johnson, vice-president and editor. "We want people who respect writing as an art."

"We ask an applicant to write a 500-word autobiographical sketch," Mims Thomason, president, explained. "Not only his finished product, but the time required to produce it, are taken into account. . . . The news agency field calls for a sense of vocation more intense than most. This . . . dedication can make agency work far more rewarding than what is reflected by union scales."

"There are no formal limitations on jobs for women, but practical considerations that limit them. Since we are a 24-hour operation, we have almost as many late night and overnight shifts as we do day shifts. We would be reluctant to assign a woman to a trick that meant she would start home at 2:00 A.M. Men generally are more flexible in accommodating themselves to late tricks."

The U.P.I. also hires experienced reporters, of course. An applicant with a good liberal arts or journalism school education, plus one or two years on a medium-circulation newspaper makes "an ideal candidate," according to Edward W. Scripps II, vice-president of Scripps-Howard Newspapers, controlling interest in U.P.I.

Only seasoned reporters—occasionally a woman like Aline Mosby, who served in Moscow and Paris—are sent to bureaus overseas. Outstanding reporters may be promoted to bureau chief with higher pay. U.P.I. bureau managers, however, must combine business with editorial work, handling office management and personnel relations and, most important, selling the service to clients.

Beginning reporters on U.P.I. are paid $5,000 a year, with annual rises to $9,880 after seven years in big cities, or $9,360 in smaller bureaus. Experienced reporters earn on the average what their opposite numbers do on most major newspapers.

QUALIFICATIONS—A.P.

The A.P. does not hire green cubs, but it, like all other employers in journalism, is seeking "youth in combination with experience."

"The A.P. has encouraged younger staffers as writers, editors and executives," says Wes Gallagher, general manager of the agency.

The qualifications for employment are the same in education, personal traits, and writing skill as on major newspapers, plus several years experience on at least a "fair-size" paper. The A.P. is looking for "fresh ideas and new talents," Gallagher says, to "broaden the news" by combining news and features. It is also emphasizing specialized reporting, surveys, and interpretation.

"Our greatest need is for editors," Gallagher says. "About 80 percent of the newsmen openings demand editing skills. In small bureaus, the news service man writes and edits his own copy. In large, relay bureaus, a large part of the staff concentrates on editing the report delivered to members.

"Most young journalists dream of becoming one of the great by-lines or columnists, but there is just as much creativity and personal satisfaction in becoming a great editor. . . ."

In pay, the A.P. minimums are within $1.25 of the U.P.I.; and above minimum, about equal.

WIRE SERVICE PICTURE MEN

The two big wire services employ many photographers, who are scattered throughout the United States and abroad, to supply the many pictures offered to clients. Their pay is about the same as reporters, except that they do not get as much as the best-paid reporters.

The U.P.I. is more hospitable to beginner photographers than the A.P., which demands some experience. The work of photographers on wire services is the same as on newspapers, except that, like reporters, they must work faster.

A.P. photographers have won the Pulitzer Prize at least five times. Joe Rosenthal took what is considered the most famous news photograph in history, the marines raising the flag on Iwo Jima during World War II.

OTHER NEWS SERVICES

There are more than a dozen other American news services, all much smaller than A.P. or U.P.I., which have fewer job openings and pay less.

Some, like Chicago City News and Cleveland Central Press, limit coverage to a local area. Some are specialized: Jewish Telegraph Agency to news of Israel and Jewish communities throughout the world, Science Service to news of science, the Associated Religious Press to church news, and so on.

Syndicates like King Features, North American Newspaper Alliance, Newspaper Enterprise Association sell columns, features, serialized books, and special articles mostly by "name" writers to newspapers. They employ a few staff journalists to edit this material. For these jobs some newspaper reporting or editing experience is generally required. Pay is about the going pay for newspapermen of equal standing in the same town.

The foreign wire services, such as Reuter's for Britain, Agence Presse for France, Aneta for the Netherlands, will occasionally hire an American journalist for their offices in the United States, or for a bureau abroad. Familiarity with the appropriate language is essential. Pay is less than on the American services.

FOR MORE INFORMATION

Ayer, N. W. *Directory of Newspapers and Periodicals.* Lists names, addresses and editors of news services and syndicates.
Editor & Publisher Yearbook. Lists names, addresses and editors of news services and syndicates. 850 Third Avenue, New York, N.Y.

BOOKLETS

Maxwell, J. William. *The Foreign Correspondent.* Department of Publications, State University of Iowa, Iowa City, Iowa. $1.
Morin, Relman. *A Reporter Reports.* Associated Press, 50 Rockefeller Plaza, New York 20, N.Y. Free. An A.P. reporter who won two Pulitzer Prizes talks of his work.

Chapter Fourteen

COMMUNITY PAPERS

SUBURBANS

A new kind of community paper, the suburban, has been booming since World War II, springing up wherever suburbs have been burgeoning in the United States. These papers make money, are housed in modern, air-conditioned buildings, are printed by the latest processes, employ large, well-paid staffs.

While they all concentrate on covering their area, "like a blanket," many also have full wire service and features, and maintain their own state and national correspondents. Even the weeklies are as big, well-written, and edited as many a metropolitan daily.

Of these suburban papers, some are dailies, not all of them new, but all with new life. There are more than 2,000 new suburban weeklies. And 1,350 "interurban" dailies or weeklies publish multiple editions for neighboring communities. All offer excellent opportunities to beginner journalists.

Among the prospering suburban dailies, *Newsday* and *Long Island Press,* competitors for the support of the 3,000,000 residents of Long Island, fastest developing suburban area in the country, are outstanding examples.

Newsday, a lively tabloid, was founded by Alicia Patterson, daughter of Joseph Medill Patterson, publisher of America's first tabloid, the *New York Daily News. Newsday* is also devoted to public service and won a Pulitzer Prize in 1954 for exposing corrupt politicians operating the local racetrack.

COMMUNITY JOURNALISM: Staff writer for Long Island paper doing story about Long Island crewmen of destroyer on patrol of Cuban waters. Reporters for small-town papers may be confined to local angles, but not the local scene. (*Long Island Press*)

The *Press*, key paper in the Newhouse chain, is older and more serious. It has its own Washington and state correspondents, and goes in heavily for constructive and provocative features on problems affecting its area.

Both these papers employ large staffs and pay wages comparable to those on metropolitan papers, though not as much as the top salaries on the biggest papers in New York, Chicago, and Washington. They demand high qualifications and suffer no shortage of applicants. They are hospitable to promising beginners. After gaining experience, many of their good staff men leave for better jobs on bigger papers.

An example of a good interurban daily is the *Bergen Record*, with seven daily editions for as many communities in suburban Bergen County, New Jersey, and adjoining Rockland County, New York.

It is amazing what big papers many of the weeklies are: staffs may number fifty to seventy-five persons full time and many more part-timers. Several hundred such papers are already coming out twice and three times a week, probably on the way to developing into dailies.

The *Ridgewood* (New Jersey) *News* prints 112 pages on Sunday and almost as much on Thursday. The *Birmingham Eccentric*, which comes out weekly in a suburb of Detroit with 64 pages, is an intelligent, good-looking publication, one of the most profitable in the nation.

The Paddock Publications put out fifteen weeklies with a total circulation of 40,000 in the northwest suburbs of Chicago. An overlapping staff of fifty editorial people produces 100 or more pages for each issue, with original magazine, sports section, women's sections, its own photographs and art work. They also take full U.P.I. news and feature service.

The Lerner group consists of twenty-three weeklies and semi-weeklies serving other Chicago suburbs. The four *Sun* papers around Omaha, Nebraska, average 68 pages each, including a staff-produced feature magazine, and circulate a total of 60,000 copies. The rising *Star* papers of Chicago Heights, Illinois, publish three semiweeklies of at least 48 pages each with 33,000 total circulation, and employ 73 people full time, 57 part time and 300 newsboys.

The seven Hartley weeklies for suburbs of Columbus, Ohio, have a uniform body of editorial page, women's page, sports page, and features produced by a single staff. But each paper has a separate outside wraparound with its own front page, society page, church and club news, produced by its own two-person staff.

Such chain weeklies and interurbans can be remarkably successful. Professor Kenneth R. Byerly of the University of North Carolina School of Journalism estimates an efficient operation grosses between $100,000 and $500,000 a year. With such an income, they are able to offer beginners salaries as good as smaller metropolitan dailies, and perhaps a brighter future.

SMALL-TOWN COMMUNITY DAILIES

There are 1,000 community newspapers published in small towns, either restricted to or primarily devoted to local news and advertising. The great majority are in old-established towns, not new suburbs; they are not expanding and cannot attract enough ambitious beginners for the wages they can afford to pay.

Some small-town dailies, however, are distinguished for good journalism: the *Emporia* (Kansas) *Gazette,* founded by the respected William Allen White; the *Belmont* (Mass.) *Citizen;* the *Watertown* (New York) *Times,* the *Alice* (Texas) *Daily Echo,* whose editor, Mrs. Caro Brown, won a Pultizer Prize for dethroning the political dictator of her county despite harsh opposition and intimidation.

A job on a community daily like these will give a youngster valuable experience and a chance to move up to the big leagues.

COUNTRY WEEKLIES

The Directory of Weekly Newspaper Representatives lists 4,400 "country" weeklies in farm areas, rural or resort towns. In general, they are not progressing; many not even prospering. There used to be 14,000 of them in the United States fifty years ago.

On rural weeklies, there is no lack of jobs for young journalists, but the pay is half the starting wage on a first-class, metropolitan paper with none of the other benefits. And your future is doubtful, unless—or even if—you buy the paper!

This does not mean you cannot practice good journalism on a country weekly. Hazel Brannon Smith, co-owner with her husband of four weeklies in Mississippi, battled for civil rights although her plant was bombed. She won a Pulitzer Prize. The late Horace W. Carter of the *Tabor City Tribune* and Willard Cole of the *Whiteville News Reporter,* tiny North Carolina weeklies, shared a Pulitzer Prize for helping convict one hundred Ku Klux Klansmen of violence.

Nor is it necessary to slay dragons to make a weekly famous. All an editor need do is give his paper personality. Henry Beetle Hough did it with his *Vineyard Gazette* of Martha's Vineyard, Massachusetts, and Orville Campbell with the *Chapel Hill Weekly* in North Carolina.

NEIGHBORHOOD PAPERS

There may be some interesting, though hardly secure, jobs on the 650 neighborhood weeklies. These are published for well-defined communities within big cities, such as the *Village Voice* or *The Villager* in New York City, for example.

There is plenty of "news" in such neighborhoods, leaning heavily on local entertainment, art exhibitions, shopping columns, real estate development, personality sketches. The support comes from local advertising.

In general, though, neighborhood weeklies are declining as cities deteriorate at the center and urban neighborhoods lose identity.

JOBS ON COMMUNITY PAPERS

The journalism manpower shortage is severe on community papers, especially on small weeklies.

Publishers want cub reporters to have a liberal arts or journalism diploma, ability to write, curiosity, enthusiasm, but they are compelled to accept beginners with less. There are always "help wanted" ads for cub reporters for community papers (the principal publications that carry them are listed at the end of the chapter). Employment agencies have hundreds of calls.

"They can't get enough people to go to small towns in the hinterland," says Rick Friedman, weekly paper editor for *Editor and Publisher*. "All the ambitious journalism graduates yearn for the Big Time, by which they mean New York or Washington."

To be happy on a community paper, a newsman or woman should be a convivial person who likes small-town life, rather than an adventurous spirit who longs for travel, excitement, contact with famous people.

Community journalism is particularly satisfactory to women who want to live in the suburbs or a small town with their families and work close to home. Some weeklies prefer women journalists as more stable, cheaper, and better suited to the work than men. Consequently, there are many women staffers, editors, and even some publishers of weeklies.

Starting salaries on community papers vary from $50 to $110 a week, depending on the size and wealth of the paper. Top wages, however, even on the best, are less than those on major papers. The editor of a successful country weekly may expect $150 a week, of a booming suburban daily or weekly $250. Added compensations are lower living costs and warmer personal relations.

Some community paper reporters pick up a little extra income by acting as stringers for metropolitan newspapers. Stringers are used for routine news and in emergencies, but when big news breaks in their area, staff reporters are sent to take over. A good stringer, however, may be rewarded with a job on the big paper.

To a cub, the value of a reporter's job on a small-time paper is the chance to gain all-around experience fast. You may learn more journalistic skills in one year there than in five on a metropolitan paper. On weeklies particularly, the newsman has a chance to do everything—all kinds of reporting, writing, rewriting, editing. He writes editorials and headlines; reads proof and makes up the paper. And he will not have the A.P. to backstop him or press agents to hand him poop.

On the smallest weeklies, the newsman may also have to solicit ads, build up circulation, even write ads for some customers.

"It is ten times tougher to be a good newspaperman in a small town than in a metropolitan area," says Alan C. MacIntosh, editor and publisher of the *Rock County Star-Herald* of Luverne, Minnesota.

The purpose of getting that experience is to qualify for a better job on a bigger paper—many celebrated newsmen started on obscure papers—or to own your own paper.

OWNING YOUR OWN WEEKLY

Many a metropolitan newspaperman has dreamed of becoming his own boss, owning his own paper in a pretty, quiet town, getting out of the rat race and going fishing on weekdays.

A few have actually realized the dream.

Ralph Morton gave up his job as foreign news editor of the A.P. in New York in 1954 and, with his wife, built the *Dartmouth* (Nova Scotia) *Free Press* to 8,500 circulation and into Canada's best weekly.

Kenneth Walker, who knew nothing about running a country weekly, bought the rundown *Colfax Chronicle* in a poor Louisiana town of 1,600 population nine years ago and began making $10,000 to $15,000 a year after the first two, hard years.

The old-fashioned country weekly was a by-product of the town job press, with the printer its publisher-editor. Both the paper and the job press are disappearing. Many of the remaining ones are in financial need and for sale.

Harris Ellsworth, newspaper broker, says a weekly paper with "backshop" (printing) equipment can be bought for $20,000 to $30,000 today, but that the return may not be worth it.

That heavy, initial investment can be avoided by having your weekly produced by modern offset, a much cheaper process than linotype and letterpress. It is not necessary to own your own offset machinery. There are plants specializing in this work, like Victor Leiker's in Middletown, New Jersey, which prints sixty tabloid weeklies. Some weeklies own one offset plant cooperatively, like Western New York Offset Press in Buffalo, which prints thirty-eight papers.

Sometimes a printer, hot metal or offset, will extend credit to a new publisher in hopes of getting a good long-term contract. Sometimes, capital can be raised from local investors.

"HE-AND-SHE" WEEKLIES

There are a number of thriving "he-and-she" weeklies, operated by married couples who are the entire, full-time staff. Journalism schools in the agricultural states prepare students for such a career. Experience as an employe on a weekly paper is a valuable prerequisite for both man and wife, and the man, at least, should have some business acumen as well as journalistic ability. And both partners should be prepared to work sixty or seventy hours a week to make a decent living.

The usual arrangement is for the man to act as business manager as well as reporter-editor, while his wife minds the office, keeps the books, and does inside editorial work.

Every weekday, the editor rides around town gathering news from town officials and merchants. He gets stories from meetings of the Lions or Rotary, or the Grange, to all of which he belongs. At the same time, he is lining up ads for the week; the bulk of his advertising is local. He takes news pictures and writes the week's editorial, perhaps a feature column, too.

Meanwhile, his wife is editing social and club notes from dozens of volunteer women correspondents, news from the high school correspondent, gathering personal items by phone. She takes classified ads on the phone and in person, helping customers to write them.

Standard features come from a syndicated service.

Wednesday is the traditional day for putting a weekly to bed. Together, the editor and his wife make up the paper and read

Opposite Page: FAMILY WEEKLY: Ed Shearer, son of owner of *North Mississippi Herald,* is editor, linotyper, pressman. His wife, Betty, is office manager. Edward III is growing up in the paper. (*National Newspaper Association*)

proof. It is printed on Thursday. Augmented by a high school boy or two, the staff wraps papers for mailing to out-of-town subscribers. Bundles are given to newsboys for home delivery and to shops. The staff takes Sundays off.

Papers of 800 subscribers earn an average of $5,000 net profit; 2,600 circulation, $9,500; 6,500 circulation, $16,000; assuming that no salaries are paid to the publisher-editors. There is no union in the picture to affect wages and hours of employes.

FOR MORE INFORMATION

BOOKLETS, PAMPHLETS, PERIODICALS

A Weekly Newspaper. Industrial Series No. 43. U.S. Department of Commerce, Bureau of Foreign and Domestic Commerce, Superintendent of Documents, Washington, D.C. 15¢

Careers in Newspaper Publishing. No. 189. $1

Careers in the Publishing Field. No. 9. $1

  Institute for Research, 537 South Dearborn, Chicago 5, Ill.

Editor & Publisher. Weekly trade paper of newspaper industry. Editor & Publisher. 850 Third Ave., New York, N.Y. 20¢

Grassroots Editor. Quarterly of International Conference of Weekly Newspaper Editors. Southern Illinois University, Carbondale, Ill.

The National Publisher. Monthly. National Newspaper Association, 491 National Press Bldg., 14th & F Streets, Washington, D.C. Trade paper of community newspapers.

The Publisher's Auxiliary. Weekly trade paper of community daily and weekly papers. 33 North Michigan Ave., Chicago, Ill.

BROADCAST JOURNALISM

Chapter Fifteen

BROADCASTING THE NEWS

The newest, most dynamic, fastest developing area of journalism is radio and television news. In considering the choice of a career, students of a certain temperament will be fascinated by news broadcasting, an exciting blend of show business and journalism.

Broadcast journalism has the same fundamental purpose of all journalism: to give the news. But its method is unique, fundamentally different from all previous journalism. And that makes radio and television news superior in some respects, inferior in others, to printed news.

THE SUPERIORITIES

One important advantage of radio is that it gets the news to the people with a speed unmatched by any other method. In the heyday of Park Row, when big news broke, the presses would be stopped, an extra run off, and the streets would echo with the excited shouts of newsboys. As radio news became commonplace, the newspaper extra fell into obsolescence and finally disappeared.

Today, everyone knows the big news long before a newspaper comes to his hand.

Through the organization and technology of electronics, Lyndon B. Johnson's election as president was accurately projected at 6:48 P.M. on Election Day, 1964, before the polls had closed in the West!

Newspapers have given up competing with radio and television in trying to break the news first. Yielding the bulletins to the

SAFELY DOWN: The Gemini 6 spacecraft with astronauts Schirra and Stafford inside is seen moments before it was lifted aboard the U.S.S. *Wasp*. This was the first time television viewers saw live pictures of a space flight recovery. The TV pictures were beamed to the United States via satellite from the recovery carrier *Wasp* located some 900 miles southeast of Cape Kennedy. (*NBC*)

electronic media, newspapers have turned more attention to expatiating details, analysis, reporting-in-depth, and features.

Television is unique in its presence, actuality, liveness beyond any other medium. Only television is literally the "eyes and ears of the people." When an astronaut takes a walk in space, the best a newspaper or magazine can do is to describe it in words and show a few still pictures. Reading cannot compare to the thrill of watching close up the man floating one hundred miles above earth and overhearing his conversation with a shipmate. On TV you yourself are right there.

Television is the only medium that can report the facts without the interposition of the reporter. When there are contradictory statements as to facts, the fair newspaper gives all versions equally, but often the reader is left in doubt as to what is the truth. Though the camera and mike cannot always be eavesdropping on news sources and events, it is only on TV that the people can ever hear and see *for themselves* what happened and what was said.

When the candid camera and mike are present, their revelations can be decisive in creating public opinion, resolving a controversy, settling an issue.

In quick, mass, public education, television is unequaled. The networks' half-hour to three-hour documentaries on problems like drug addition, water shortage, population explosion, Negro leadership, American foreign policy are superb reporting-in-depth. This form is being used more and more, becoming better and better.

THE LIMITATIONS

Curiously, the greatest advantage of television is also an inherent weakness—the dependence upon pictures.

Many important news stories can be told best in words, but words without pictures are held to one minute or less on TV. There is nothing duller than watching a man reading a text to you.

Where it is impossible to get film, either because the camera could not reach the scene in time or because it was barred (as from a court trial or session of Congress), the news item is ticked off in a sentence or two. News that is not amenable to picturization—such as "dope" stories, obits, personality sketches, texts of reports, reviews of books and music, explanations of scientific discoveries—is all but ignored.

HISTORY OF BROADCAST NEWS

Broadcasting is such a modern method of disseminating news it is hard to imagine what will supersede it.

Radio news was made possible in 1895 when Guglielmo Marconi invented wireless telegraphy. However, the first news broadcast was not made until November 7, 1916, when Lee De Forest, inventor of the vacuum tube, transmitted returns of the Woodrow Wilson–Charles Evans Hughes election from New York to a few ham operators.

Using words instead of "dits" and "dahs," radio news developed rapidly in the next thirty years. At first, newspapers fought the new competition; but, failing to lick 'em, they joined 'em, buying their own radio stations.

It was during World War II that radio realized its full potential as a news medium by instantly bringing word of the Munich Pact, Nazi blitzkreig, bombing of Pearl Harbor, of crisis after crisis, day after day. People hung over the fateful box, silent and intent, at home, in restaurants, in automobiles, for the latest word. The newspaper lost forever its traditional rôle of town crier.

At that time newscasting became a profession. Great reputations were made by the late Edward R. Murrow, William L. Shirer, H. V. Kaltenborn, Eric Sevareid, Elmer Davis, and others —mostly newspapermen—who entered the new medium. The networks and larger independent stations organized full-time news departments.

Sight was added to sound in 1923 when Vladimir Zworykin perfected the iconoscope tube. There was no television news broadcast, however, until 1939, when President Franklin D. Roosevelt was seen on screen opening the New York World's Fair. This was followed in the next few years by occasional telecasting of prearranged events, like the national conventions and football games, to a few thousand receivers in existence. World War II virtually halted television; radio had broadcast news to itself.

But as soon as war restrictions were lifted in 1947, TV began an explosive growth. By now, the screens are flickering in approximately 90 percent of American homes and surely 100 percent of barrooms, nearly sixty million sets in all.

At first, radio sets were decimated, then the transistor revived the medium. Now 97 percent of American homes have a radio; there are millions more in cars, offices, factories, shops, and stores, not to mention countless tiny receivers carried about by some people who never allow one moment of silence to descend upon us.

Broadcasting into this vast receivership are 3,500 AM and 775

FM radio stations and 675 TV stations at this writing, though un-doubtedly there will be more by the time you read this.

Certainly television has not reached the end of its development. On the horizon is Ultra High Frequency, which will more than double the number of channels. Like its FM radio counterparts, UHF will extend TV broadcasting to small budget, noncommercial stations, which can specialize in quality programs of music, news, and discussion. This will mean more and interesting jobs for broadcast journalists.

EXTENT OF BROADCAST NEWS

Every radio and TV station broadcasts some news. Even the smallest radio station will give a five-minute summary every hour, a fifteen-minute roundup in the evening and perhaps also in the morning.

Since the big entertainment shows have gone to TV, radio has turned increasingly to music and news, adding such quasi-news as advice to homemakers, sports events, discussion of public questions, service information like weather and traffic conditions.

Larger radio stations give as much as six total hours of news during their broadcast day; a few, like WNEW and WINS in New York, have recently gone on a continuous schedule of news and features twenty-four hours a day every day in the year. The time, money, and effort put into news by television also is being constantly enlarged.

Nearly all TV stations belong to one of the three nationwide television networks. Many, but not most, radio stations belong to one of the four national or eighty regional radio networks. Affiliated stations in both radio and TV take most of their national and international news from their network for rebroadcast.

The three major networks—National Broadcasting Company, Columbia Broadcasting System, American Broadcasting Company —which are both radio and television, provide about twelve hours of news and features out of a broadcast week of eighty-four hours to 200 to 300 stations each. A fourth national network, Mutual Broadcasting System, which is radio only, supplies thirty news programs a day to 500 stations.

As an example of an active regional network, the Yankee Network gives a total of six hours of news a day to thirty-six stations in the New England area.

A typical schedule of a major network will include a half-hour of general news each evening, one hour of news features each morning, a one hour documentary on a current question each week (such as NBC's "White Paper" series, CBS's "Reports," ABC's "Scope"), and one or two half-hour or full hour interviews or discussions each week.

In addition, there will be 160 or more special news programs that come up during a year. When President Kennedy was assassinated, for instance, the networks cancelled everything else, including commercials, and remained on the air with that news and its aftermath fifteen hours a day for four straight days.

The largest independent stations provide their own substantial news programs. In radio, these rival the output of the networks.

Big, local affiliates of networks produce about as much local news as they receive from their networks. When broadcast "back to back" at dinner time, these programs may amount to one to two hours of news, with local items emphasized during the first portion and general, national, and foreign news in the latter portion.

Chapter Sixteen

JOBS FOR
BROADCAST NEWSMEN

Broadcasting is not a big field of employment. The Television Information Office estimates there are only 43,000 full-time employes of radio stations and 32,000 of television stations in the entire country. The average radio station has less than fifteen workers, and the average TV station less than fifty-five. The four, big national radio networks employ a total of 1,000 persons and the three nationwide TV networks 9,000.

Only a small fraction of the total broadcast employes are newsmen, because, although all stations broadcast news, only a minority cover it themselves.

A survey of 2,677 young men and women who graduated from journalism schools in 1965 turned up only 74 who found jobs in radio and 85 in television. Of 15,820 journalism students of all kinds, only 709 were studying major sequences in radio and television.

These data do not, however, accurately reflect the annual entry into the broadcast field, since many recruits come not directly from colleges but from the ranks of working newspapermen.

As news operations of radio and television are constantly being increased, more jobs will appear in the future. However, the number of stations is not increasing, so the United States Department of Commerce expects new jobs of all kinds in the industry to be created at the rate of only 2,000 a year. Of these, possibly 200 will be newsmen. Ultrahigh-frequency is not expected to make a great change in the employment outlook since most of the stations will be small.

TV is typically a big city job. Seventy percent of all TV jobs are in cities of over 100,000 population; but 60 percent of all radio jobs are in smaller centers. Twenty-five percent of all broadcasting jobs are in New York and California. New York City and Los Angeles are the principal centers of employment, followed by Chicago and then the larger cities of Texas, Pennsylvania and Ohio.

NEWS ON SMALL STATIONS

The smallest stations (Category 9) have no newsmen on their staffs. The announcer simply tears the hourly, five-minute, radio news summary off the A.P. or U.P.I. ticker and reads into the microphone the first seven or eight bulletins, interspersed with commercials and station announcements, leaving a net of three and one-half minutes of news.

If a local program is desired in addition, a reporter from the local newspaper may be hired part time to write a ten-minute summary of community news that can be read on the air at breakfast or dinner time. The quality of this local news may be judged from such typical items as the high school lunch menu, automobile accidents from the police blotter, catches of fishing boats in the harbor.

Some small, though not the smallest, stations have a news staff of one, all-around man. He rewrites the bulletins from the wire service teletype and also items of community news from the local paper. If he has enough time on the air for a feature, he may tape an interview with a town official or interview a visitor live in the studio. He then broadcasts the entire news show himself, including commercials. Indeed, he may also have to go out and hustle the commercials to realize his salary!

NEWS STAFFS OF MEDIUM-SIZE STATIONS

A medium market-size radio station may employ two or three newsmen, who will share all the duties. A small TV station may require its only reporter to handle the camera as well as the tape recorder.

The news staff is increased not only with the category of station (determined by power of transmitter and population reachable), but also with its interest in covering news. A staff of any size will include cameramen, lab technicians, perhaps a film editor. An active news staff will have at least one mobile unit—that is, a truck with sound camera, generator, lights, reflectors, all equipment to broadcast live from the field, such as the scene of a fire.

SOME TYPICAL OPERATIONS

Here are a few setups and operations typical of the broadcast news field outside of the big networks, as cited by the National Association of Broadcasters:

(1) A top power, radio-TV station in the Northeast has nine reporter-rewritemen and three cameramen handling the two major newscasts on TV daily through Saturday and one on Sunday, plus five fifteen-minute radio newscasts, two ten-minute radio newscasts and half a dozen five-minute summaries daily.

(2) A TV station in Florida has twenty-two men, including a day editor, night editor, two newscasters, eight cameramen-reporters, three lab technicians, a film editor and a film librarian. It operates four moble units. It produces one ten-minute and two fifteen-minute news shows and two ten-minute sports shows daily.

(3) A top power radio-TV station in a big Midwestern city employs thirty-four persons in news, including a director, a TV news editor, a radio news editor, an assignment editor, special events director, sixteen newswriters, three two-man camera crews, two film editors. They produce four fifteen-minute TV shows each weekday, two half-hour TV local summaries on weekends, and a dozen newscasts from five to fifteen minutes each daily.

In addition, here are some other stations, outside the major networks, that are important in the news field:

KNX, Los Angeles, biggest news broadcaster outside New York City, employs twenty-four newsmen. WOR, key station of the small Yankee Network, has seventeen newsmen in New York and an equal number of staff correspondents elsewhere, including foreign countries. WQXR, owned by *The New York Times,* and WINS, operated by the Hearst chain, are notable among the many broadcast stations that are owned by newspapers. They use the paper's reporters as occasional broadcasters as the day's news may indicate, and thus have available a large staff without employing them full time.

NEWS STAFFS OF NETWORKS

The largest employers of newsmen are the three major, nation-wide networks. Of these, the two giants, Columbia and National, each have about 500 men and women full time in their news divisions; American has fewer. Roughly half of each force are editorial workers, while the rest are manual workers, technicians, engineers, clerks, administrators and so on.

The three big networks compose the big leagues of broadcast news. They do the most comprehensive and professional job, employ the best newsmen, pay the highest wages. Since all three have headquarters in New York, a majority of their newsmen are stationed there. Washington, of course, has a good number of resident correspondents. The rest are stationed throughout the world or jetting about on short missions.

A NETWORK STAFF ORGANIZATION

Of the 250 editorial employes on a network news division, about 170 will be assigned to television and 80 to radio. Some correspondents and some other employes are put to work interchangeably between the two media.

The network also has on call a large number of stringer correspondents, who are usually newsmen employed full time on an affiliated station. These are used as occasion demands for a particular job and are paid on a fee basis.

The news division is headed by a president or vice-president who corresponds to the managing editor of a newspaper. Under him are a man in charge of television news and another in charge of radio news. Each of these has assistants. All these top-level executives correspond roughly to assistant managing editors; indeed, all have had impressive experience on newspapers or in news broadcasting or both.

The working news staff is organized differently from that of a newspaper or news magazine. Each "show," whether a regular, five-days-a-week news summary, a late evening roundup, a morning feature program for housewives, a weekly documentary in series, or a special, one-shot feature, is set up as a unit.

Each show unit is headed by an executive producer, who has under him a staff of fifteen to thirty journalists and about an equal number of cameramen, soundmen, other technicians, craftsmen, and clerks. The editorial men include associate producers, directors, editors, writers, researchers, reporter-contact men, copyreaders, film editors, sound editors, correspondents.

When unexpected news breaks that requires a special show outside the regular schedule, as, for example, Pope Paul's visit to New York in 1965, a special "task force" is put together for the purpose. Its makeup is similar to that of a regularly scheduled "show" team.

THE NEWSROOM

The newsroom of a network or of a large independent radio or TV station rather resembles the city room of a newspaper. It has a similar clutter of paper-strewn desks, the same clatter of typewriters and teletypes, the same chatter on the telephone, the same shirt-sleeved informality. As in a newspaper, most of the staff sits together in the open room without private offices, each man concentrating on his own work as best he can.

In plain sight from every desk is a big wall clock with a running second hand, for time is the thorn in the side of every electronic newsman. There is one unique fixture—on the wall a bank of three television screens constantly monitors not only that network's output but also the output of its competitors.

A similar battery of TV screens is constantly running in every executive's private office. The important men even have this set of multiple screens, perhaps several sets, at home. They say they don't mind living with this eternal bedlam, but to an outsider it seems a hellish torture.

In the newsroom, a skeleton staff is on duty at all times. Each man works an eight-hour day, although the nature of news may

Above: TV NEWSROOM: It resembles newspaper city room. But on wall are receiving sets constantly monitoring its own broadcast and those of competing networks or stations. (*CBS*) Below: ASSIGNMENTS: From this desk, men are assigned to cover major stories around New York City. The deskman is in touch with all correspondents and film crews via shortwave radio between the news desks and the newsmen's cars and mobile units. (*NBC*)

require frequent overtime, of course. It takes about eight hours to put a half-hour news show together. The main staff will come to work about 11:00 A.M. for a show that goes on the air at 7:00 P.M.

DUTIES OF EACH JOB

Assignment Editor   Assignments, local, national and foreign, are made by an assignment editor. Ninety percent of the spot news on radio and TV originates on wire service tickers and in the daily newspapers. Very rarely do you see an exclusive spot news story of any importance on the air. However, you do see many exclusive features and documentaries on current topics. Ideas for these come from correspondents, from press agents who want to publicize their clients, and from editors themselves. Thinking up such ideas is an important part of the editor's job.

The television assignment editor must always keep in mind one vital consideration which the newspaper editor can ignore— visualization. Is there film in it that will tell the story? The ideal TV story tells the news without one word from the newscaster. The astronaut floating in space, Jack Ruby shooting Lee Oswald in Dallas Police Headquarters are examples of perfect picture stories.

Every TV newsman, whatever his job, should have a film sense. A good news story without good film will not get the relative play on TV which it gets in a newspaper.

When the assignment editor decides to cover a story, he dispatches a crew to the scene. The minimum crew consists of two men—a cameraman and a reporter. A full crew may include one or more cameramen, a soundman, a light man, a number of other hands, and the reporter-contact man.

Reporter-Contact Man   The reporter-contact man is in charge of the crew and the job. His work is analogous to that of a newspaper reporter, but there are differences, too.

The newspaperman can go to work instantly, anywhere, with a pencil and notebook. He can stand silently aside, watching, listening, taking notes, or he can roam freely, interviewing a dozen persons informally to gather facts for his story.

The television reporter is accompanied by camera and tape recorder, perhaps also lights, reflectors, power cables, the equipment that Fred Friendly, former president of CBS News, calls our "one-ton pencil." It is not always possible to take that one-ton pencil into the scene of news. Then people in the news must be brought out to the equipment.

It is the reporter-contact man who must get them, set the stage for the interview, discussion, or statement. He not only handles the microphone and does the interviewing, but, like a movie director, he also directs the filming and sound recording, trying to capture a candid-camera, documentary, unstaged feeling. All the time he is making notes to guide the script writers and editors in the home studio. Finally, he must see to it that the film is put onto a plane, or taken to the nearest lab for processing and then to a studio for transmission to headquarters as fast as possible.

Cameramen Just as every TV reporter ought to have some picture sense, so every TV photographer must have some news sense. The next time you watch TV news, pay attention to the camera work.

If the reporter, off-screen for the moment, is describing a flood, the film may open on a wide shot of Main Street under water. Do you notice the building sign, "Riverville National Bank"? The photographer picked that shot to "establish" the locale.

While the reporter is interviewing survivors and rescue workers, the camera roves from closeups of the speakers to the swirling river, to children being carried off a floating house, to refugees, and back to the speakers—the pictures always keyed to the words, yet never riveted too long on one thing.

Reporting with film takes considerable skill. Some journalism schools give courses in it, and so do some schools of photography.

Opposite Page: REPORTING WITH FILM: Color television cameras cover the Mass celebrated by Pope Paul VI during his visit to New York in 1965 at Yankee Stadium. (*NBC*)

In the end, however, it must be learned by apprenticeship to good men on the job.

TV Editors   In the newsroom, the editors take the film and cut it into the news program. It is always cut.

The anchorman may say, "For that story, we take you now to Mike Rafone in Kashmir." You then see Mike briefly and hear him talk for one or two minutes while the camera shows turbaned soldiers fighting in the Himalayas. The crew in the field may have shot 3,000 feet of film that would take forty-five minutes to roll. To snip that big spool to 200 feet or less is the fearful job of the editorial editor and the film editor. Working together, they see to it that the news is told properly and dramatically. They cut not only for content but also for technical quality.

The editorial chief has the responsibility of deciding how much of each film and story to use on a show. Sometimes he faces the dilemma of a top story with poor or no film, and great film with a less important story. Then he consults the film editor, director, newscaster, chief writer and, with their aid, makes his decision. In the end, he may be overruled by the producer, who is the top man.

Broadcast Writers   Meanwhile, the writers are pounding out the basic script. News writing for radio or television is not exactly like news writing for a newspaper. It is, first of all, very much briefer. What a newspaper takes a column to tell, the TV or radio program clicks off in eight lines. The writing is also simpler, more informal, more relaxed. There is no desire for striking prose.

Most radio news writing is straight rewrite of wire copy. The writer scans ten, twenty or forty news stories as they come over the ticker, selects the most important and rewrites them into the show. If the news does not change before the next broadcast, he faces the problem of rewriting the same stuff to make it sound fresh. If fresh news does break, he must write a new top for the show and drop something out. In an eight-hour stint, he may handle fifty items.

Television writing is more conversational than radio writing, since the narrator is seen as well as heard. Full sentences are not always required. To key his words to the film, the TV writer must either view the film or consult a "spot sheet," which is a summary description, scene by scene. On each story, he writes a lead-in, rather than a newspaper lead, and also a summary conclusion, which, ideally, bridges over to the following item.

Radio scripts are typewritten in measured lines, TV scripts in half-lines. In an accompanying column are capsule descriptions of the scene and/or sound, which are cues to the newscaster to help him keep his comments in step with the film. In another column is the time each item should take and the log of accumulated time. Reading at the standard rate of 2 to 2½ seconds per half-line, the newscaster must keep the show on schedule.

The newswriter's script is edited by a copyreader, who does much the same job as his opposite number on a newspaper, except write headlines. The copy is edited again by the editor, and a final editing is given by the newscaster himself. It will be seen, therefore, that the task of radio or television newswriter is hardly one for a wordsmith, a prose artist. It is always teamwork, always anonymous, and rarely distinguished.

The writer of a radio or television documentary has more time and more opportunity to express himself, to coin a phrase. He also gets credit on camera or on the air for his authorship. But even documentaries are always contributions of more than one man and are heavily edited by editors and newscaster.

Researcher   Facts for a documentary or big special news feature are gathered by researchers. A network may employ forty of them—mostly bright girls. Their work is similar to that of researchers on news magazines like *Time*. They gather and check facts by interviews in the field and by digging in libraries.

Correspondents   Correspondents are the top reporters, the men you hear on the air and see on the screen. Some are identified with a particular news show, but all appear occasionally on other, special shows as well. Most double in radio and television where a station or network serves both.

A network or a big independent station like WOR may have fifteen to forty correspondents.

Whether they work out of the home office or far away, they are all called correspondents. Some are on general assignments and are sent out on big news stories anywhere in the world—to Winston Churchill's funeral in London or to Brazil on a documentary about agricultural development of the Amazonian jungle. Others are specialists in affairs of state, labor, art, theatre. Some are Washington correspondents. Many are foreign correspondents on fixed stations abroad, although their tours of duty in any one place are much shorter than the usual three-year hitch of newspaper correspondents.

A correspondent's work is similar to that of a newspaper correspondent's, which is why former newspapermen are preferred. The main difference is that the broadcast correspondent must be able not only to cover and write a story but also to deliver it into a mike and before a camera. In the field, he must also act as the reporter-contact man and make all the physical arrangements for the entire crew's work.

Anchorman   The star of a news show, the chief correspondent, the newscaster who speaks the body of the news and who introduces the other correspondents for one- or two-minute spot reports, is called the "anchorman." The show's popularity depends so much upon his personality that he gets billing in the title— "The Huntley-Brinkley Report."

People say, "Walter Cronkite said last night . . ." But the work of sixty researchers, reporters, writers, and editors went into what he said. Most of them remain anonymous, though a few names may be flashed on the credits at the end of the show.

Director   In broadcasting, the title "director," is used for two quite different jobs. The news director is the man in overall charge of the operation of broadcasting news, even on a tiny radio station with a staff of one. In networks and large stations, each news show also may have a director in charge; this is an executive job.

ANCHORMAN: Walter Cronkite is central newscaster for
CBS Television news show every weekday evening. Such
top jobs pay $100,000 or more a year.

Each news show also has a technical director. Like a movie
director, he calls the shots for film, voice, sound, switches the
projection from full view to closeup, devises background stills
called "telops." Stopwatch in hand, he or an assistant calls cues,

speeds or slows things, cuts things out, keeps film and voice coordinated.

Unfortunately for the technical director, it is not possible for him to rehearse a news show before it goes on the air. When you consider how rarely the announcer's words fail to coincide exactly in time and content with film, you appreciate his skill. Since his primary object is to project news, he must have a news sense, as well as a dramatic one.

Producer   The producer is the executive boss of the show, as has been indicated. He is responsible for everything—the content, presentation, hiring the personnel, the cost.

THE LINEUP

Two to four hours before the news show goes on the air, the lineup session is held. This is analogous to the daily news conference of editors in a newspaper. The chief writer, the chief editor, the director, and the newscaster go over together all the material in hand and expected, discussing the relative time and emphasis to give each item and in what order. They arrive at a tentative schedule so that the writers, film cutters, map and chart makers, et al can go to work on the show.

Changes, of course, are made right up until show time as required by late-breaking news, by film that does not arrive in time or comes in bad, by other emergencies sure to occur every day.

WHAT IT TAKES TO MAKE A BROADCAST JOURNALIST

The requirements of broadcast journalists are the same as for newspapermen—and more.

The education demanded is the same: a broad, general, college education. Undergraduate vocational courses, acceptable to many newspaper employers, are not valued at all by broadcasting executives. Graduate courses in broadcasting are acceptable but not demanded.

Previous newspaper experience is always desirable. On networks and larger stations, it is demanded. But not all, or even most, good newspapermen make good broadcast newsmen.

"The correspondent must have not only the reporter's skills but also the ability to project believability, seriousness, intelligence, dignity on the air or screen," explains Ralph Paskman, assistant director for TV news of CBS. "He must have the face, voice, manner to convince an audience he knows what he is talking about and has a serious interest in the subject. He must be able to think fast on his feet, ad lib in spot interviews and fast-breaking events. He must be alert; quick yet relaxed; deliver without stuttering, hemming and hawing, repetition, or nervous tics. He must use good (but not pedantic) grammar, diction, and taste, speak well without any regional or class accent, and not like an actor."

Television editors, both of words and film, must have an eye for pictures, as well as a nose for news. They also must have special skill at cutting, far beyond that required of a newspaper editor. To snip two hours of video tape down to thirty seconds without losing the essential story requires a talent that perhaps not everyone is born with.

To be a producer takes all the qualities of the reporter, writer, editor and technical director—in other words, the ability to put on the show. And many producers will actually take part in the writing, editing and directing. It is not surprising that they are men of indefatigable energy. It is said that Fred Friendly, who produced the one-hour documentaries "CBS Reports," went into the film-cutting lab on Friday afternoon and lived there, constantly at work, until Sunday night.

Broadcast news executives unanimously advise beginners to work a few years as a newspaper reporter and then to begin their broadcasting career on a small station. Work on a small station gives wide experience in the business quickly. The all-around newsman will have to function as reporter, writer, editor, newscaster, perhaps cameraman, soundman, film editor, director and producer.

"In no other branch of journalism does a newsman require such a broad range of skills," says one network director.

After he has gone through this spectrum but still early in his career, the young broadcast newsman should decide whether he wants to become a writer, a correspondent, or an editor. If he has ambition to become a producer eventually, he should take the editor's route, since producers rarely develop from the reporter-writer-correspondent group.

Broadcast jobs tend to divide into on-camera, on-air or off-camera, off-air; into word men or picture/sound men; into creative jobs like reporter, writer, correspondent, or production jobs like editor, director, producer. Seldom can a career, once in motion on one track, be switched to another.

The four national radio networks and three national television networks, all with headquarters in New York City, are the goal of all broadcast newsmen.

These networks and some of the largest local stations as well never employ beginners right out of college as newsmen. All their writers, reporters, correspondents, editors, directors, producers have had experience on newspapers or smaller broadcasting stations for at least five years, and many for much longer. The networks demand not only experience but superior ability besides.

Even researchers at the networks have had some comparable experience on news magazines or in big libraries.

Once in a while, NBC will take on an interne to learn the business, but he is rarely rewarded with a permanent job there, even if he turns out well. More likely, a promising youth will be farmed out to a small, wholly-owned station of the network for seasoning. CBS takes some beginners out of college for the lowest, manual jobs like copyboy, messenger, camera grip, and so on.

WOMEN IN BROADCASTING

Prejudice against women in broadcast journalism is worse than on newspapers; 70 to 90 percent of the editorial staff is male.

Most job opportunities for girls are in research, but no station below medium size can afford a researcher, and below network level research staffs are always small.

Women have become film cutters and film editors, assistant directors and associate producers of news shows. Some have gotten jobs as reporters, writers and editors. A few have become full-fledged correspondents. Pauline Frederick, Aline Saarinen, Nancy Dickerson, Jeanne Paar, among half a dozen on the Big Three networks, are all mature journalists who made their reputations on newspapers.

Broadcasting executives deny prejudice against female journalists.

"We have more women in editorial jobs than our competitors," boasts Julian Goodman, vice-president of NBC News. "We have no prejudice against women and do not stick them with so-called women's specialties exclusively. We have at least one woman news producer, and a number of correspondents who do general work like the men."

"We are looking for good women reporters all the time, but we cannot seem to find any qualified," laments Mr. Paskman of CBS. "They would have to be smart, well-informed, capable, and good-looking without being affected or disturbing. We are accustomed to hiring men as correspondents, and possibly unconsciously accept lower standards for them."

Nevertheless, women journalists consider themselves as good as men on the air or screen, and assert they are unfairly barred by male executives.

SALARIES IN BROADCAST NEWS

The average starting salary of journalism graduates in radio news in 1965 was $100.38 a week, in television, $90.67, less than same as on daily newspapers. Beginning wages on the smallest stations approximated those on the smallest weekly newspapers, about $70 a week. And like the reporter on a country weekly who has to sell ads, the newsman on the little broadcasting station may have to sell commercials to make his pay.

"A good TV reporter on a small station in a small town may earn half of what a rewriteman earns on the local paper," says Harry Reasoner, CBS correspondent and former newspaperman.

"At the networks, all reporters, writers and editors earn more than their counterparts on any newspaper."

Surveys indicate that women's pay averages $10 a week less than men in the equivalent job, purely because of sex prejudice.

Wages in general rise with the size of station and of the city, but even within one city there are wide variations. For instance, one radio station in Chicago pays newsmen $90 a week, another $142.

Copyboys and clerks at the networks in New York start at $65 a week, almost as much as a newsman makes on a small radio station in a country town. Researchers on the networks start at $150 a week.

On the networks and many larger stations of both radio and television, some minimum wages are set by contract with two unions. The Writer's Guild of America bargains for newswriters and deskmen, the lower grade of editors. The American Federation of Television and Radio Artists bargains for reporters and some correspondents. The highest paid correspondents, however, are exempt from any union regulation of wages and hours.

In New York, Writer's Union minimums for newswriters include these: NBC, $160 a week to start, $224 after two years; CBS, $155 to start, $205 after two years; WOR and WINS, $170 to start, $215 after three years; WNEW, $165.50 to start, $231 after three years. Better writers are paid above minimum.

Editor is a higher paid category than newswriter. A broadcast deskman, corresponding to a newspaper copyreader, would start in a big city at about $200 a week. The union minimum in New York is now $247. Many editors make much above this.

AFTRA members rank higher than Writers' Guild members. Kenneth Groot, executive secretary of the New York local of AFTRA, estimated recently that base pay of news reporters throughout the country varied upward from $125 a week on small, rural stations.

In New York, the AFTRA minimum for reporters varies all the way from $140 to $425 a week, depending upon whether they appear on camera or are heard on the air and how often. The base pay for those appearing on network news programs of fifteen minutes or less, five days a week, is $331, for instance.

This base pay is augmented considerably by "talent fees" for performances on camera or on the air in excess of the minimum, either on the same or additional programs.

Premium pay for overtime is also provided.

Pay of a news director may vary from $4,000 a year on a small, rural station where he is the whole news staff to $30,000 a year on a New York network, according to the Radio-Television News Directors Association.

Producers of news shows, despite their high-sounding title, can start as low as $15,000 a year, well below the pay for some of the "talent" on their staff. However, in New York they can make $50,000 or even $100,000 a year.

Wages of correspondents are determined in individual bargaining, whether they belong to AFTRA or are exempt, as long as they do not fall below the union minimum. Probably no national network correspondent gets less than $15,000 a year, some perhaps $100,000. Star anchormen like Walter Cronkite are said to earn "a couple of hundred thousand a year."

FOR MORE INFORMATION

National Association of Broadcasters, 1771 N Street, N.W., Washington, D.C.
Television Information Office, 666 Fifth Ave., New York, N.Y.

BOOKLETS, PAMPHLETS

Broadcast Education. Annual list of courses in broadcasting in colleges of U.S.A. National Association of Broadcasters. Free.
Broadcasting the News
Careers in Radio
Careers in Television
   All free from National Association of Broadcasters, 1771 N Street, N.W., Washington, D.C.
Career Interne Program in Broadcasting. Requirements, examinations, pay, etc. for beginning broadcast journalists on Voice of America, available from Employment Branch, U.S. Information Agency, Washington, D.C. Free

Angel, Juvenal L. *Careers in Television and Radio.* World Trade
    Academy Press, 50 East 42nd St., New York 17, N.Y. 26 pp. $1.25
Employment Outlook in Radio and Television. Government Printing
    Office, Washington, D.C. 10¢

PERIODICALS

Broadcasting Magazine. Monthly. 444 Madison Ave., New York, N.Y.
Radio-Television Daily. 1501 Broadway, New York, N.Y.
Television Magazine. Monthly. 444 Madison Ave., New York, N.Y.
Television Quarterly. National Academy of Television Arts and Sci-
    ences, 54 West 40th St., New York, N.Y.

4

WIDER FIELDS OF JOURNALISM

Chapter Seventeen

BIG, BRIGHT, MAGAZINE WORLD

The newsstand in the railroad station is shingled with magazines, tier on tier covering every inch, hundreds of magazines competing with bright covers to catch your eye and coins, more magazines than you thought existed, some you never heard of.

Yet, this big, bright display is only a sampling of all the weekly, fortnightly, monthly and quarterly publications shuffling out of the presses in this country. If you anticipate a career in magazines, you have chosen an enormous field.

The total number of magazines in the United States has been estimated at 16,000 to 20,000. There is scarcely any occupation, hobby or recreation, any religion, philosophy or political view, any society or group, any human activity or interest that does not have a magazine devoted to it.

Professor Roland E. Wolseley, chairman of the magazine department of Syracuse University School of Journalism and author of standard reference works, gives this approximate grouping:

Consumer magazines of general interest, 250; magazines of special interest, 4,250; religious magazines, 1,500; business publications, 2,500; house organs, 8,000.

The small but important group of general interest magazines, appealing to the "broadest segment of the population," includes many of the most popular, national magazines like *Reader's Digest, Saturday Evening Post, Life, This Week, Harper's.*

The specialized magazines range over an endless variety of subjects and include some of the biggest books in the country as well as little, nonprofit magazines with part-time editors. Included in the specialized group are more than ninety news magazines, of which *Time* and *Newsweek* are leading examples; women's magazines like *McCall's, Vogue, Ladies' Home Journal;* homemaking magazines like *Good Housekeeping, Better Homes and Gardens;* sports magazines like *Yachting, Sports Illustrated, Outdoor Life;* juvenile magazines like *Boy's Life;* magazines like *Farm Journal* for farmers and their families; magazines for parents, do-it-yourselfers; magazines concerned with science, astrology, art, literature, travel, health, education, nature, everything from antiques to zoology.

Virtually every fraternal, patriotic, educational and other organization of any size publishes its own magazine. A notable few of them, like the *American Legion Magazine* and *National Geographic Magazine,* enjoy large circulations also among the general public. They make money from advertising and employ big, well-paid staffs.

Though most religious magazines are subsidized and use clergymen as part-time editors, some, like *Catholic Digest, Christian Herald* and *Commentary,* are thoroughly professional publications with wide prestige. The field offers interesting work to dedicated journalists who are not primarily seeking high pay. In addition to the 1,500 publications in magazine format, there are 200 religious papers, mostly weeklies and biweeklies.

The prosperous business publications, devoted to a particular trade or industry or to business in general, offer excellent opportunities to young journalists. They are discussed in Chapter Eighteen.

Accounting for half the total of all magazines, house organs of individual business concerns compose a huge area of potential careers, greatly under-valued by beginners. This field also is separately treated, in Chapter Nineteen.

Taken all together, magazines blanket the nation, reaching 90 percent of all American families. The circulation trend parallels that of the national educational standard—a 101 percent increase in high school graduates in the last ten years was matched by an equal rise in magazine distribution.

The consumer magazines alone distribute four and a half billion copies a year. The forty biggest national periodicals have a circulation of more than one million each, the greatest, *Reader's Digest,* fifteen million in the United States, twenty-five million in fourteen languages over the world.

Although there are bigger, more successful magazines than ever before, the magazine business is highly competitive and therefore not so stable as the newspaper business. The leading national magazines are always locked in deadly combat for readers and advertising. Some front runners inexplicably fall back, even die quite suddenly, while others storm up from the rear to take the lead. In this fight, staff members may lose jobs through no fault of their own, and whole staffs may be wiped out.

TAKEOVER BY JOURNALISTS

Magazines have become one of the major vehicles of journalism since World War II. A generation ago, popular magazines based their major appeal on entertainment, light fiction and humor, and on pretty pictures. Interest in the short stories and serialized novels that used to "sell the book" has dwindled under the preoccupation with more gripping events in the real world.

While entertainment still exists in popular magazines, the major attraction today is more likely to be an article of fact or explanation, an interpretation of current affairs, discussion of topical issues—in other words, material produced by journalists.

"Nonfiction, which in prewar years was only one-third of the average content of magazines, now exceeds the quantity of fiction two to one," Paul Swensson of The Newspaper Fund reports.

Some all-fiction magazines died. In the general field, the change in policy of the *Saturday Evening Post*—from six short stories, two installments of novels and two articles in a former issue to six articles and two stories today—is typical. The women's magazines, once dependent on sentimental love stories and romantic verse, now lead every issue with serious discussion of a public or individual problem of the day—abortion and sterilization, urban planning, race relations, mixed marriages, sex and the single girl. The "quality" magazines, which used to provide a market for literary fiction, are fewer than ever. The survivors, like *Harper's* and the *Atlantic Monthly*, print only one or two short stories per issue, giving all the rest of their pages to articles of fact and opinion.

Journalists have benefited, not only by more space, but more jobs, too, because, while fiction is always contributed by outsiders, one-half to three-quarters of nonfiction is written by staff members.

REPORTS-IN-DEPTH

Once they turned to journalism, magazines realized they were ideal vehicles for reporting-in-depth. All go in heavily for it now, and have lured some of the best reporters in America away from newspapers to their staffs by higher pay and more interesting work.

The news weeklies began as nothing but summaries of what had been in newspapers of the past week, and their staffs were mostly rewritemen. Now, they have a large staff to do original reporting, and each issue features a "cover story," that is, a report-in-depth of some topic or personality in the news.

The picture magazines like *Life* and *Look* now give half their contents to text, mostly in-depth articles done by journalists. The *Saturday Review* was a languishing book review until Editor Norman Cousins gave it new life as a weekly of current discussion.

THE MAKING OF A MAGAZINE

"The making of a magazine is a creative process," Carroll J. Swan pointed out in a recent brochure of the Magazine Publishers Association. "It requires the imaginative talents of writers and artists and layout experts . . . the abilities of those who know how to organize and stimulate creative people. Here is a business that relentlessly, issue after issue, demands new ideas be developed, expressed, presented, a bundle of intangibles with a broad reach into the minds of millions. . . ."

New ideas for articles are the key to success in the magazine business. Anyone on the staff, from office boy to publisher, is

STORY CONFERENCE: Magazine editors, with their assistants, meet regularly and often to plan issues, sometimes months in advance. (*Time Magazine*)

free, indeed urged, to contribute such ideas. The most prolific and ready source of article ideas is the daily newspaper. If from that and any other source you can come up with ideas that win popular approval among your readers, you will move up the staff fast. Try to get a job on a magazine that you yourself would read even if you did not work there. Then you will identify with your readers.

It is not only staff members who contribute article ideas to a magazine. Some come from free-lance writers looking for assignments, others from readers, others from public relations men seeking to promote a client. Magazines also hire professional researchers to find out what readers want.

Once the idea is accepted as possible, the editor talks it over with his staff. He checks it against similar material already published or ordered. He considers in what issue it would best run. If the idea passes all tests, he assigns the story either to a staff member or a free-lancer he knows.

SIZE OF STAFFS

On a very small magazine, the editor alone, or perhaps with the aid of a "gal Friday," has to procure his articles from outside writers, write some pieces himself, edit all the material, obtain pictures and write captions, make up the pages, read proof, oversee the distribution. And, all the time, run the office too!

Time magazine, at the other extreme, has a home editorial staff of 250, including 49 writers, 13 editors, 66 researchers. In addition, it has 102 staff correspondents and 291 part-time stringers throughout the world. *Life* has a home staff of 125, including 20 writers, 12 editors, 12 researchers.

Here is a typical table of organization of a monthly magazine, somewhere in the middle-size range, as given by Mr. Swan:

The editorial department employs fifty out of a total headquarters staff of two hundred. At the top is an editor, under him an executive or managing editor. The editorial staff is divided into three branches—art, editorial production, editing-writing. The last (which interests us most) is subdivided into three groups—fiction, nonfiction articles, and "service" columns and regular features on such things as fashion, new equipment, letters to the editor.

The journalistic jobs in the magazine field (though not all may

MAGAZINE LAYOUT MEN: Art and production editors plan and diagram the pictures and blocks of text on every page. (*Life*)

be on any one magazine) are editorial assistant, researcher, reporter, copyreader, writer, assistant editor, senior editor. Sometimes job titles and duties are combined: as researcher-reporter, reporter-writer.

EDITORIAL ASSISTANT

Standing a little above clerk or secretary, the editorial assistant helps the editor she is assigned to in every way short of actual writing for publication or exercising editorial judgment. On big books, the job puts your foot on the lowest rung of the editorial ladder; on smaller magazines it is a "gal Friday" job for secretaries.

RESEARCHER

A researcher gathers and checks facts for writers and editors. News magazines like *Time* employ big staffs of researchers; most other large-circulation magazines, too, employ one or more. It is a job for bright, young, college graduates without experience. Almost all researchers are girls; a few magazines, *Life*, particularly, occasionally hire young men with ambition to learn the business from the bottom up.

There is a chance for talented, determined, young women to advance from researcher to copyreader, reporter, writer or even editor. But generally, a researcher remains one until she gets married and quits in two or three years. Those who don't quit often grow into senior librarians.

An example of the painstaking work a researcher does is given by John Reddy of the *Reader's Digest*. An article on the Bank of England, run by the *Digest* in March, 1964, contained this paragraph:

> Ever since the Gordon riots of 1780, when two unsuccessful mob attacks were made on the Bank, the Old Lady has been protected by a "picquet" of 12 Guardsmen led by an officer, a sergeant, two corporals and a piper or drummer.

These were the research check questions: Were the riots called

Gordon riots? Spelling of Gordon? Did they take place in 1780? Were there two attacks? By mobs? Were they unsuccessful? Should Bank be capitalized? Is it called Old Lady and capitalized? Has it been protected continuously since 1780 by Guardsmen? Are there 12? Is picquet the correct term? Should it be in quotes and is it spelled correctly? Are the Guards led by an officer, a sergeant, two corporals and either a piper or drummer?

REPORTER

Reporters' jobs exist mostly on news magazines, though some general magazines also employ a few reporter-researchers. The reporter's function is not exactly like that on a newspaper. The magazine reporter may not write a line for publication. He, or more likely she, will interview news sources and gather facts in the field; then write a memorandum for the staff writer who will do the article. It is a job for beginner-writers and should lead to a full writing job on the same or another magazine.

COPYREADER

A magazine copyreader does not have the power a newspaper copyreader has to change a writer's story. She ranks below the writer. The magazine copyreader is limited to correcting errors of fact, syntax, making changes to conform to the magazine's style of punctuation and spelling, correcting proofs. Substantive changes are left to editors. Editors also, not copyreaders, write headlines on magazines.

Unlike newspapers, magazines hire many women as copyreaders. They don't sit together at arc-shaped desks either. Each copyreader has her own desk and works alone.

WRITERS

The Magazine Publishers Association estimates that three-fourths of all material published in magazines is staff written. On news magazines, 100 percent is staff produced. On house organs, business publications, technical and many specialized magazines, most of it is.

Most of the "service" departments and regular features on the general magazines are turned out by staff members. Fiction is always contributed by free-lancers. Many of the articles are too, but more of these than you think are inside jobs. For instance, out of the fifteen original articles in each issue of the *Reader's Digest*, more than half are written by the seventeen roving staff editors or by so-called free-lancers who have an arrangement for frequent assignments.

On the mastheads of many magazines you will find no "writers" listed. That is because magazine staff writers are usually titled editors. There are actually writing editors and non-writing editors.

Magazines demand more personality, individuality, "literary" talent of their writers than newspapers do of reporters. Even news magazines make this demand.

"Youngsters who ask me for writing jobs are nonplussed when I want to see any poetry they may have written for their college papers," says Martin O'Neill, senior editor of *Time*. "But I can tell more from that than from their news stories. The same compression, imagination, turn of colorful phrase, hitting the nail on the head, required of poetry is required for news writing on *Time*."

Time once hired a young writer to do movie reviews on the strength of satirical sketches he had written for the New York nightclub, Upstairs at the Downstairs.

Unlike newspapermen, magazine writers are not required to be objective. On the contrary, they must arouse the sympathetic emotions of their readers, whether by amusing, shocking, thrilling, titivating, comforting or advising them.

Previous newspaper experience is not required by a magazine. Some editors feel that newspaper reporters do not make good magazine writers because they are bound to facts and trained to objective statement. They are also used to writing a story once, fast, and letting it go. Magazines polish a piece over and over again.

"Every story is the work of several, perhaps many, men and women," says one editor. "They have contributed ideas and facts to it, written and rewritten it, edited it, until it is quite un-recognizable from the original."

The great Mike Berger quit a higher paying job on *The New Yorker* after one year and returned to *The New York Times* because he could not endure endlessly reworking an article he had written as well as he could the first time.

EDITORS

No one is called a rewriteman on a magazine, although an enormous amount of rewriting is done. Junior editors rewrite articles contributed by outsiders, particularly public officials, celebrities, authorities whose by-lines and knowledge are indispensable but whose journalistic skill is inadequate. Some natures find it frustrating to write or rewrite completely an article that will be published under the by-line of the mayor, the President's wife, or an atomic scientist.

Senior editors rewrite junior editors. On *Time,* an article may be rewritten by a half-a-dozen men as many as twenty times.

Top echelon editors neither write nor edit. They do give the final reading and criticism. Their principal duty, however, is to initiate ideas.

The principal quality demanded of magazine journalists—as distinct from newspapermen—is creative imagination, expressed in fresh ideas for articles and illustrations, and original approaches to familiar topics. The outstanding magazine articles create a sensation, not by breaking news but by their bold handling, such as *Life* magazine's picture story of the birth of a baby, or *Reader's Digest's* "And Sudden Death," detailing the horrors of automobile accidents.

"An editor should also have a sixth sense of timing," says John K. Herbert, president of the Magazine Publishers Association, "that instinctively knows the propitious time to feature a story, a subject or author."

YOUR CHANCES ON MAGAZINES

In magazines, as in other areas of journalism, there is a surplus of jobs.

The American Council on Education for Journalism recently estimated that 7,000 of our magazines employ 66,000 men and women, about one-fourth of these being editorial employes. However, only 5 percent of the 1965 journalism graduates chose jobs on magazines, including house organs.

"Our problem is not finding jobs for our graduates who have majored in the magazine area," reports Professor Wolseley, "but in finding students available for the jobs. Men or women who take the pains to get out résumés, answer ads, follow our leads, and wake up to the fact that house magazines and other specialized ones pay better for beginning jobs than do the big books, can have three or four to choose from. Most of the jobs come from specialized magazines. Opportunities for graduate students are even better."

Though most of the big books require previous magazine experience, some of the biggest, like *Time, Newsweek, McCall's,* take on a few journalism school graduates as editorial trainees and some students as summer internes. They are engaged for three, six or twelve months to learn the ropes by doing research, reading manuscripts, assisting with makeup or layout. Those who show promise may be permanently hired. In any case, the experience is an asset in applying for a job elsewhere.

On news magazines, beginners are almost always hired as researchers. They can progress to become copyreaders or writers, eventually editors.

"On *Life*, we also hire a few young newspaper reporters with four or five years experience to be reporter-researchers in the hope they will develop into our kind of writer," says Thomas Carmichael, assistant to the managing editor. "We look for good feature writers rather than hard-news writers. One characteristic of our work is that you must write and edit with picture possibilities always in mind."

Journalism graduates can start right out on smaller magazines as staff writers or editors. On specialized publications the graduate who has been educated in an applicable subject will be especially welcome.

One of the best, though most difficult, ways to get a staff job on a big magazine is to write for it free lance. *Reader's Digest* selects its staff mainly from among its contributers.

Time magazine selects its writers mostly from among its 291 stringer correspondents, who are reporters on local newspapers. They have a chance to progress to staff correspondents, editors, and senior editors. Senior editors are never hired but are "grown" inside the organization, according to Roy Alexander, managing editor.

A peculiarity of employment on big national magazines should be mentioned. When a new top editor is appointed, particularly to revive a fainting magazine, he brings with him his team of top subordinate editors. That means the former team is out looking for new jobs, and that vacancies have been created by the new team's evacuation of their old jobs.

WOMEN ARE WELCOME

There is no discrimination against women on magazines except on the highest executive level. Magazines generally do not share newspapers' concern about female editors directing male staff members. A large number of women have held top editorial posts ever since Sarah Josepha Hale began producing *Godey's Lady's Book* before the turn of the century.

There have been female magazine war correspondents like Martha Gellhorn and photographer Margaret Bourke-White, and peacetime foreign correspondents like Dora Jane Hamblin who served *Life* in London and Paris, was chief of its Rome bureau, and directed a combined *Time-Life-Sports Illustrated* team covering the Olympics.

Possibly 60 percent of all magazine journalists are female. The ratio among recent journalism graduates who go directly into magazine jobs is about 53 percent.

One outstanding magazine executive has special advice for women eager to make a start on a career on the big books.

"Learn shorthand and perfect it," says Herbert R. Mayes, former president of *McCall's*. "Most college girls turn up their noses at secretarial work, but they can always get into a big magazine that way. Once they're in, they can see how the magazine does things, what it wants. They can suggest story ideas personally to the editor, show their talent for writing or editing, become an editorial assistant. It is a lot quicker, more direct than building up a reputation on smaller magazines."

MAGAZINE SALARIES

Magazine salaries average the highest in journalism. The Newspaper Fund found the starting wage of 1964 journalism graduates who went into magazines (including house organs) to average $115.87, surpassing that in all other media and even in public relations and advertising.

However, magazine wages vary widely. The Newspaper Guild does not have contracts with most magazines. It does have contracts with most labor publications, the biggest news magazines, and two dozen specialized magazines of various kinds, mostly in New York.

Though the sampling is small these contracts give some idea of minimum salaries on magazines. They show trainees getting $53 to $82 a week to start and up to $100 after three years; editorial assistants, $88 to $107 to start and up to $128 after four years; researchers, $85 to $101 to start and up to $137 after five years; writers, $95 to $147 to start and up to $225 after four years; editors, $130 to $147 to start and up to $240 after four years.

But minimum scales have even less practical application on magazines than on newspapers. Everyone who makes good is paid above the minimum. The going wage of a magazine writer with five years' experience is put at $12,500 by the American Council on Education in Journalism.

On *Time* and *Newsweek* writers start about $200 a week and go up from there; senior editors may earn $40,000 a year. Writing editors on big general books like *Life* make from $15,000 to $20,000 a year, senior editors twice as much. Editors on *McCall's* and *Redbook* earn anywhere from $10,000 to $60,000 a year.

James R. Kobak, a leading magazine accountant, found that salaries of editors of consumer magazines range between $24,000 and $40,000 a year. One woman editor of a fashion magazine got

$42,000, and one editor of a general consumer magazine $70,800, which was more than his president!

FOR MORE INFORMATION

BOOKLETS, PAMPHLETS

Career as an Editor and Careers in Editorial Work. No. 118. $1
Careers in the Publishing Field. No. 9. $1
   Careers Research Monographs. Institute for Research, 537 South Dearborn, Chicago 5, Ill.
Swan, Carroll J. *Magazines in America.* Magazine Publishers Association, 444 Madison Ave., New York 22, N.Y. Free
This Is Meredith's. Meredith Publishing Company, Des Moines, Iowa. Free.
Where Ideas Get a Head Start. Magazine Advertising Bureau, 444 Madison Ave., New York 22, N.Y. Free.
Wolseley, Roland E. *Careers in Magazines and Books.* Quill and Scroll Foundation, University of Iowa, Iowa City, Iowa. Free.

REFERENCE MANUALS

Ayer, N. W. *Directory of Newspapers and Periodicals.* Names, addresses, editors, circulation of about 9,000 magazines in U.S. and Canada. Lists by geography and specialization, but no description.

The buyer of a style-setting Madison Avenue men's shop in New York favors blue suits this spring instead of the grays he bought so heavily last year.

That's news—and not trivial either—to men's clothing manufacturers and merchants across the country. If other buyers follow the leader, millions of men who shop on Main Street and in suburban shopping centers will want blue suits this season.

A better synthetic rubber is developed for tires, tractor sales rise sharply, computers cut inventory handling costs for electronics distributors, a new package increases cereal sales, a new process boosts petroleum production—all that is important to some segment of American business.

Twenty-five hundred publications, 35 percent more than the number of general interest daily newspapers, cover every facet of trade news. Their readership totals fifty-two million persons. The business press is a vast, growing, prosperous field of opportunity for young journalists. Salaries are attractive, and there is a crying need for qualified writers and editors.

All publications providing specialized information to those in a particular line of business, trade or profession are called "businesspapers"—whether turned out daily on newsprint in newspaper format or as monthly, slick paper magazines in four colors. As a matter of fact about 2,300 "businesspapers" are in magazine format.

"They give to men of business and industry general news of

their field and specialized know-how of their jobs," a spokesman for the American Business Press points out. "They penetrate every corner of the economy, distributing, interpreting, analyzing this know-how as fast as it sprouts. They are the lines of communication within and across industry and business.

"Inside these publications you find no comics, no crime, no sex stories, no politics, no sports. They are not read for amusement, but for learning and information."

Each industry from advertising to woodworking, each trade and profession has its own journal, sometimes several. More than 150 categories are covered, almost always with self-explanatory titles: *Architectural Record, Iron Age, Oil and Gas Journal, Printer's Ink, Hospital Management, Hotel Monthly, Medical Economics.*

In addition, there are "horizontal" publications, which cut across industry lines to give general news of business—*Business Week,* the *Wall Street Journal, Fortune, Journal of Commerce,* and many more.

The number of business publications has been growing by about fifty a year for the last ten years; and while this rapid growth may slow, no authority expects it to drop below thirty a year before the end of the century.

Some business publishing houses have themselves become big business.

McGraw-Hill publishes daily papers for the construction industry in Phoenix, Chicago, Denver, and San Francisco; and forty magazines as various as *American Machinist, Chemical Engineering, College and University Business, Nursing Home Administrator, Purchasing Week,* and *Today's Secretary.* The company employs 700 full-time editors and 595 part-time correspondents located all over the world.

Fairchild Publications produces three dailies with big circulations: *Daily News Record,* covering men's and boys' wear; *Home Furnishings Daily,* and *Women's Wear Daily;* as well as five weeklies giving news of drugs, electronics, footwear, metalworking, supermarkets, respectively, and a bimonthly, *Men's Wear.* Nine hundred and eighty-four correspondents (601 full time) staff the worldwide Fairchild News Service. Three hundred and eighty-four reporters work in New York, thirteen in the Washington bureau (one of the largest in the nation's capital); and the rest work out of thirty-nine other bureaus in marketing and production centers in the United States and thirty-three foreign countries. There are major bureaus in Paris, London, Milan, Frankfort, Yokohama, Bombay, and other leading cities. Fairchild is the third largest American news agency, surpassed only by The Associated Press and United Press International.

The business press as a whole employs more than 70,000 people, of whom 14,000 have editorial jobs.

TALENT SEARCH

Constant growth and a hesitation by young people to enter business journalism keep the business press on an unceasing search for talented, ambitious young journalists. As far back as 1958, the Standard Rate and Data Service found that 60 percent of business publishers were having difficulty in finding acceptable editors.

As a result, the field offers starting salaries and opportunities for advancement beyond most newspapers. A typical career timetable is described by Walter L. Botther, publisher of Standard Rate and Data Service:

"A capable college graduate entering a business publication house as an editorial assistant in his early twenties could normally expect to become an assistant editor by the time he is thirty years of age, an associate editor at about thirty-five, managing editor in his forties."

Salaries average $4,250 to $5,500 as an editorial assistant; $4,700 to $13,500 as a reporter and staff writer; $4,400 to $14,600 as assistant or associate editor; $8,200 to $18,000 as managing editor; $12,000 to $28,000 as chief editor or editorial director. On some prosperous business publications, writers receive $16,000; assistant editors, $24,000; top editors, $35,000 and up; publishers, $65,000 to $90,000.

"On many publications, salaries are augmented by insurance and medical programs," Mr. Botther adds. "In addition, more progressive publishers are instituting profit-sharing and pension plans."

A survey by Bernard Gallagher revealed that half of the business publishers had instituted incentive plans by 1958. Recently some have distributed options allowing key executives and others to buy company stock at less than market prices.

Yet, many journalism graduates with magazine majors "turn up their noses" at jobs on the business press because they think it lacks glamor, according to Professor Wolseley. They all want to work on the great national magazines like *Life* and *The New Yorker*.

But, since the great national magazines employ very few beginners and have an enormous surplus to choose from anyway, there are far more—and frequently better—jobs for inexperienced young people on businesspapers.

"The value of starting on a small publication," Professor Wolseley says, mentioning the business, science and education fields in particular, "is the opportunity to gain varied experience performing many different operations. If there is a desire to move to a larger magazine, this then is a possibility. Often, however, that desire wanes, and a fine career is built by staying in the specialized area."

IS IT DULL?

But isn't the work, the life dull and routine?

Authorities in the field shout, "No!"

"Business press editors roam all over this country and the world to cover international conventions, business crises, wars, catastrophes, and other news stories in their fields," says Donald A. Moser, an associate editor at McGraw-Hill. "The editor finds himself the friend, confidant and adviser of government, business, theatrical, scientific leaders."

Moser estimates that McGraw-Hill editors travel an aggregate of four million miles a year, making nearly 5,000 calls at plants, laboratories, and offices to obtain material for articles.

Fairchild has one or two reporters covering every presidential news conference; one is assigned to every major government bureau in Washington; and there have been Fairchild News

BUSINESSPAPER EDITOR: They also go out on stories. Here one enters a new diving bell for article on undersea drilling. (*McGraw-Hill*)

Service seats in the Congressional press galleries for the last thirty-five years.

You may see a *Women's Wear Daily* reporter at the races at

Le Mans, at a fashion opening in Florence, at a smart party at Ochos Rios. *Women's Wear* critics review foreign movies abroad before critics here have a chance to see them.

Such on-the-spot coverage is provided increasingly by all sectors of the business press. Their subscribers have come to demand complete, accurate, firsthand reporting.

Of course, as in any other field, the apprentice must serve his time. Hired as a general editorial assistant, the beginner may help one editor after another until he learns the ropes of the entire operation and finds out what he does and likes best. During this period, he may write picture captions, rewrite minor releases, read proof, help make up, do research, and some original reporting.

The apprenticeship usually is short. If the tyro shows promise, he will soon get stories of his own to write.

VALUE OF THE WORK

The good businesspapers not only provide information with dollars-and-cents value to people in their industry, they also make contributions to community service. Many have subsidized and initiated original research, have campaigned for reform laws and government regulation.

The *Wall Street Journal* is proud of its public service. Its staff members have won Pultizer Prizes three times in the last five years. Norman C. Miller, a young reporter, won it in 1964 for exposing a multi-million-dollar fraud involving loans on nonexistent corn oil. The same paper founded The Newspaper Fund to improve journalism education and recruit better talent into journalism.

Above all, the information disseminated by the business press is vital to industrial progress of our civilization.

WHAT BUSINESSPAPERS WANT

Most businesspapers want applicants with bachelor's degrees; a few in highly technical fields ask for a master's and even a doctor's degree. Some of the latter insist upon specialized education or practical experience in the field.

However, it is a curious fact that, more and more, the demand is for writing and editing skill above vocational knowledge. This is true even in engineering and electronics. An electronics magazine editor admitted he had to change his hiring policy when he realized that his best stories were being brought in by staff members with no training in electronics. It is well known that there is an inverse relation between technological and literary aptitudes; there are not many civil engineers who can write.

Nevertheless, specialized knowledge is always a valuable asset. Some publications send young staffers back to college or technical institutes after office hours to get it. Others provide on-the-job courses to acquaint the journalist with techniques and working conditions in the industry.

If you as a student are aiming at a certain quarter of business journalism, it might be valuable to take an appropriate course or two in college, such as science, economics, or business administration, while you are majoring in journalism.

But do not neglect your liberal arts education. Julien Elfenbein stresses this in his authoritative book, *Business Journalism:*

> The businesspaper needs men and women who are intellectually mature and curious. They must know how a contemporary society operates and what its problems are. The men and women we need must not only be educated in the specialisms of the communications industry, but also in the liberal arts, the ethical and social sciences, and in citizenship as background for the privilege of operating or directing our type of comunications' lines.

YOUR OWN BUSINESSPAPER

Can you start a little businesspaper of your own and make it go?

Howard and Barbara Katzander, a husband-and-wife team of journalists who did it, say, "Yes—IF—you find a vacuum first."

The Katzanders, both then on the Sunday staff of *The New York Times,* had bought a town house and were hunting for eighteenth century antiques to furnish it. It was while haunting the showrooms of auction houses in New York that they found their vacuum. There was no way to tell what a piece of antique furniture or a picture was worth.

"Woudn't it be useful to know?" the Katzanders asked art and antique dealers on Manhattan's East Side.

"It certainly would," was the universal answer. "How could it be done?"

The enterprising couple conceived the *International Art Market,* a photo-offset monthly magazine that gives the description and price brought by every important picture, sculpture, piece of furniture sold at auction in the major rooms of the United States, England, and France. Though the Katzanders had no previous experience as publishers, their magazines is widely quoted and a financial success.

Those eager to rush forward should be warned that instant success by amateurs is rare. True, new businesspapers are started every year, but not by tyros. A recent survey showed that men starting their own publications were comparatively young, between thirty-five and forty-five, but they had had from fifteen to twenty years' experience on magazines, usually in the same or adjacent fields.

A would-be publisher ought to know something of the business as well as editorial side of publishing. He ought to have enough capital for the long build-up of subscriptions and advertising to establish his publication solidly in the black. And he must have the stomach to endure the worries and tension inevitable in highly competitive business.

FOR MORE INFORMATION

American Business Press, 205 East 42nd St., New York, N.Y. Operates placement service for college graduates seeking editorial jobs on businesspapers. Publishes your "position wanted" ad in monthly "Employment Roundup."

BOOKLETS, PAMPHLETS, PERIODICALS

Career Opportunities in the Business Press. American Business Press Inc., 205 East 42nd St., New York, N.Y. Free.

Technical Writer. B-3OR, Career Briefs. Careers, Largo, Fla. 25¢ each.

REFERENCE MANUAL

Ayer, N. W. *Directory of Newspapers and Periodicals.* Has separate listing of trade journals.

Chapter Nineteen | INDUSTRIAL JOURNALISM

The production of house organs is called "industrial journalism," because most of them are put out by large industrial companies to promote goodwill among employes, customers, or stockholders. However, the term is also applied to publications of nonindustrial institutions such as hospitals, universities, museums, insurance companies, banks, state departments of highways and conservation.

The total number is estimated anywhere from 6,000 to 10,000. Some come and others go every year, though the net is probably growing. Con Gebbie's *Directory of House Organs* lists 4,000 of the most solidly established.

This is another branch of journalism not to be overlooked as a career possibility.

THE QUALITY VARIES

House organs vary in format from single-sheet, multi-lithed newsletters ground out by a public relations man in his spare time to handsome magazines professionally written, beautifully illustrated, as wide-ranging in subject matter as a national consumer magazine.

You may have seen some of these quality books: *The Lamp*, published by the Standard Oil Company of New Jersey for stockholders and employes; *Ford Times*, pocket-sized monthly handed out to car buyers through Ford dealers; *Arizona Highways*, put out by the highway department of that state.

Only a small part of the space is given to promotional material and this is so subtle you cannot object to it. *Ford Times,* for instance, runs travel articles and color prints of original paintings of resorts without mentioning Ford cars, though a Ford may occasionally appear in an illustration.

A general rise in the journalistic standards of house organs has been noted in recent years. As in other branches of journalism, there is less emphasis on trivia, more on serious material.

If you become the editor of a house organ of a cereal manufacturer, for instance, you are likely now to give less space to employes' marriages, engagements, bowling scores and more to new industrial processes, new uses for plant by-products—articles that take journalistic skill to develop.

HOUSE ORGAN CIRCULATION

About half the house organs are produced for employes or members and are called "internals." One-fourth are "externals," produced for outsiders, such as dealers, customers or stockholders; and one-fourth are both internal and external in circulation.

A few externals boast huge circulations; the *Chevrolet Friends Magazine,* for instance, distributes 2,000,000 copies per issue.

Giant corporations like General Motors, General Foods, General Electric each produce several kinds of house organs for various divisions of the company.

There are publishing companies that put out chain house organs on contract for concerns like savings and loan associations. These are little quarterly magazines with a uniform body of short articles within a special wraparound devoted to promotion of the particular bank buying that edition.

WORK CONDITIONS ARE GOOD

The staff of a house organ is often part of the public relations department. Many are one-man operations. The editor plans each issue, writes it all or solicits contributed articles, takes pictures, lays out, makes up.

At the other end of the scale, a big, fancy house organ may employ a dozen or more staff writers and editors. Some, like *Ford*

Times, pay professional free-lance writers and painters up to $500 for an article or pictures.

There is more opportunity for beginners on house organs than on any other kind of publication. Even the best of house organs take them. There are always "help wanted" ads in newspapers for house organ editors; employment agencies have jobs waiting to be filled. Professor Wolseley says he cannot come close to supplying the demand from employers for journalism graduates to edit house organs.

Beginners get responsible assignments of writing and editing immediately and full responsibility very soon. The work is leisurely and the conditions usually very pleasant.

"My job," says a young woman editor, "is no less 'journalism' than chasing two-alarm fires—and is more interesting and pays as much, too!"

Rapid staff turnover on industrial house organs aggravates their need for recruits. Those on the inside insist that this does not reflect dissatisfaction with the job, but it is the result of rapid promotion from the staff to more important positions within the company. They point to many former house organ editors who have become vice-presidents in charge of public relations, some, top-rank administrative officers.

Apparently, not many house organ editors grow old in the job. A recent survey by the International Council of Industrial Editors showed that two-thirds of them were under forty years old.

Though women are not the majority of house organ editors, they are increasingly accepted. One survey estimated there are now five women industrial editors to eleven men, a rate it termed "comparatively good." Women suffer some discrimination in salary, however.

PLUS AND MINUS

Wells Huff, past president of the International Council of Industrial Editors and editor of three house organs for the LaClede Gas Company, makes this assessment of the job of house organ editor:

"Why is it a good life? The most important factor is that industrial journalism presents its own challenges and satisfactions of doing a specialist's work. When it is well done, the editor has the reward and the appreciation of his associates and his readers.

"The practitioner, unlike the newsman, has a larger share of responsibility—often the whole responsibility—of seeing his publication through from conception to printed result. Within his own company, he has a freedom few other employes have. . . . He moves throughout the organization, talking to people . . . and gathering the information and ideas he needs. At a given moment he is as likely to be talking to the president as he is to the lowest-salaried, newest employe.

"There are disadvantages, too," Mr. Huff admits. "As opposed to general circulation publications, the industrial press is necessarily rooted in the affairs of the sponsoring companies. It is primarily concerned with news and features of special interest to employes or customers or other special 'publics.'"

Since almost all house organs are distributed free and do not carry advertising, their budgets depend upon their value to their sponsoring companies as public relations instruments. It follows that the biggest, richest companies will pay the highest salaries to house organ editors.

Some pay as much as $20,000 a year to staff editors; lesser companies as little as $100 a week. Some house organ editing jobs are farmed out to newspapermen to do in their spare time. The latest survey by the International Council of Industrial Editors showed more than 20 percent of the full-time editors earning $10,000 a year or more.

WHAT YOU NEED

More than half the industrial editors interviewed believe that formal journalism study is a requisite for the job. About 40 percent hold journalism degrees.

Courses in news writing, picture taking, magazine production, layout and design are especially recommended. Previous newspaper experience is not required, except for top jobs on the big house organs.

What special characteristics ought a house organ editor to have? Listen to Wells Huff again:

"The industrial editor needs the ability to get along well in his company; he must balance the objectivity of a practicing journalist with the loyalty and respect of an employe for his organization."

Naturally, he must become familiar with business and, as Mr. Huff emphasizes, "not just business in general but *a* business."

FOR MORE INFORMATION

International Council of Industrial Editors. Jim Craffey, chairman of education committee, c/o IBM Electric Typewriter Division, 545 Madison Avenue, New York 22, N.Y.

REFERENCE MANUAL

Gebbie's *Directory of House Organs.* Con Gebbie Press, New Paltz, N.Y.

Chapter Twenty

PUBLIC RELATIONS
CAREERS

A suburban weekly on Long Island included an eight-page supplement this afternoon. It contained twenty-six "news" stories, some more than a column long, all timely, lively and well-written.

A sampling of the headlines illustrates the variety of subjects:

WAR ORPHANS GO TO COLLEGE

L.I.R.R. TAKES JOB OF HATCHING DUCKS

JOB CORPS NOW RECRUITING

LIGHT IS SOURCE OF ENERGY FOR PLANTS

MORTON HUNT WRITES OF SOUND

STATE RECEIVES WILDLIFE FUNDS

BILL PENALIZES VANDALS' PARENTS

All twenty-six stories are publicity releases, written not by reporters for the paper, but by men and women engaged in public relations. The writers may be called press representatives, press agents, press secretaries, public relations directors, P.R. men or women, public relations counselors, news bureau directors, publications coordinators, supervisors of information research, or managers of media relations. One amusing characteristic of the profession is the invention of such titles.

No matter what they were called, all these men and women did their job so well that the editor could use their releases "as is."

Probably few readers realized this "news" had been written to cast favorable notice upon: the Veterans Administration, Long Island Railroad, U.S. Job Corps, Pennsylvania State University, a new book, the U.S. Department of the Interior, and legislation desired by the Long Island Home Builders' Institute.

"The job of public relations, in the broadest sense, is to earn goodwill," say Walter W. Benson and Richard J. Shepherd, two experts in the field. "This means doing good and letting people know about it."

To let "people know about it," P.R. men and women produce and place news, feature stories, and opinions in newspapers and magazines, on television and radio, or assist writers and editors to do so. In other words, they also practice journalism.

But with one important and unique difference. Journalists employed by the media are supposed to handle a story on its merits, disinterestedly, with no pecuniary involvement. Indeed, it is unethical for a staff writer to take money from anyone he writes about; most papers will summarily fire a reporter who does so. A public relations man, on the other hand, is legitimately paid and obligated to handle a story for the benefit of his client or employer. The newspaper or magazine knows for whom he is working and can accept or reject his free contribution for what it is.

P.R.'S CONTRIBUTION

Public relations men have made themselves quite as indispensable to newsmen as to their clients, but only by producing legitimate news and background.

There is little space or air time today for such stunts as plopping a circus midget onto J. P. Morgan's lap at a Senate hearing or having a show girl ride a white horse into a hotel lobby. Such high jinks have gone out even among theatrical press agents.

It is safe to say that no newspaper in America could come out today without the aid of press agents. For better or worse, they have become one of our regular sources of news.

Most of the news in your daily paper was given to reporters by public relations men—in fact, though not in the form in which you read it. Every department of our government, city, state, and national, right up to the White House, every foreign government, the United Nations and other international agencies, every sizable corporation, institution, association has someone authorized to speak to the press. In big organizations, it is difficult to get news except through that spokesman.

When a Washington correspondent has a question for a public official, he calls the press secretary, who arranges the interview (and usually sits in to see that the official doesn't blow it!)

When a reporter needs information from a business concern, a university, a large hospital, he calls the public relations department, which gives him the answer in the name of the top executive. The reporter may never have spoken to the man he quotes.

How is a reporter able to cover a scientific conference at which a dozen papers are delivered simultaneously in separate panels? A press agent provides abstracts of all the papers.

A reporter assigned to a dinner meeting will receive from a press agent the texts of speeches in advance so the story can be written and set in type before the soup is served. While the reporter must check the actual delivery, he knows the text is okay because the press agent has probably written it for the speaker.

The war correspondent goes out on a feature story, but he gets the general news of each day's action in a mimeographed communiqué from an Army public relations officer at headquarters in the rear.

Public relations men turn up in places that would astonish you. In disasters, press agents arrive on the scene with the Red Cross, utility companies, Coast Guard or Army engineers, to coordinate information. Without them, reporters would hop about like sparrows to pick up what scraps they could.

Even the Vatican has public relations priests in various languages.

Personal press agents are indispensable to ambitious politicians, theatrical and sports stars, and many other public figures. In our society, it is not public opinion that creates a celebrity, but the celebrity's press agent who creates public opinion. One of the earliest and greatest P.R. men, Ivy Lee, changed the public image of John D. Rockefeller, Sr., from "robber baron" to the world's most generous philanthropist.

Publicity men do not wait for reporters to come to them. Most of the news they give out originates with them. Every day tens of thousands of mimeographed "news releases" are poured out by public relations men to newspapers—tiny weeklies as well as metropolitan giants—to radio and TV networks and independent stations, to magazines, large and small. In New York and a few other big cities, releases also come over P.R. tickers in the media offices.

"Handouts" on the ticker or on letterheads of known public relations firms, of official bureaus, legitimate business concerns or institutions are generally respected by editors as trustworthy.

Publications with inadequate staffs print good publicity releases with little or no changes. Bigger publications turn them over to staff writers to rework by finding new facts and taking out the tub-thumping.

Writing and sending out releases is not the only way to publicize a client. Public relations men are also busy setting up press interviews and conferences, arranging press previews of new shows, buildings, and products, grinding out background material to help reporters covering news stories.

COMPETITION FOR SPACE

The competition for free space and air time is so keen that publicity news and features must present timely, interesting material to win acceptance. If circumstances do not hand a news story to him, the press agent must create it. The item about the Long Island Railroad, for instance, was born in the mind of an ingenious P.R. man, who arranged the exhibit of hatching duck eggs in the first place.

Of equal importance to creating news is the P.R. man's duty of getting it into print or onto the air. To that end, he makes "contacts" with reporters, editors, newscasters, gives them tips on exclusive stories, entertains them as much as they will allow. One of the reasons public relations firms seek to employ newspaper-men is because they have friends on the papers.

P.R. IN MAGAZINES

The extent to which magazine articles are generated by public relations men is not realized by the general reader.

"Without the help of public relations specialists, whose services are paid for by individuals or groups seeking a favorable press, some magazines would not be nearly so useful as they are," the Magazine Publishers' Association frankly admits.

Business magazines are filled with articles about successful companies, travel magazines about fabulous resorts, entertainment and sports magazines about rising stars, general magazines about fascinating personalities of the day. If you concluded that a public relations man suggested, or at least assisted with, all these stories, you would not be far wrong. That is not to accuse P.R. men of corruption and magazines of venality. The writer turns to the press agent as the obvious source of information, and the latter is glad to help in return for a kind word about his client.

The process of procuring that word can be subtle. Here is an example from the authors' own experience. One of us had been covering for *The New York Times* an investigation by the New York State Attorney General of profiteering by cemeteries. Henry Hillman, then press secretary to the Attorney General, suggested an article about such gouging all over the country for a national magazine. He provided data for a memo and interested an editor with whom he had a personal connection.

The resulting exposé, "Ghouls in the Graveyard," made a considerable stir, paid the writers well—and included an account of what Hillman's boss had achieved in New York.

WHAT A P.R. TYRO DOES

To understand what your duties as a beginner in public relations might include, read this comprehensive description by the Public Relations Society of America:

The junior employee will answer calls for information from the press and the public, work on invitation lists and details for a press conference, escort visitors and clients, help research and write brochures, deliver releases to editorial offices, work up contact and distribution lists, scan newspapers and journals, paste clippings in scrapbooks, brief his superior on forthcoming meetings, help write reports, speeches, presentations, articles and letters, research case histories, help produce displays and other audio-visual materials, do copyreading, select photographs for publication, arrange and guide plant tours, perform liaison jobs with advertising and other departments, arrange for holiday and other remembrances, conduct surveys and tabulate questionnaires, work with lettershops and printers.

WHERE THE P.R. JOBS ARE

The 1960 Census counted 30,359 persons engaged in public relations in the United States. The number is undoubtedly much larger now, since the occupation is rapidly growing.

The greatest concentration of public relations jobs is in business and industry. Three-fourths of the 300 greatest companies have public relations departments now, as compared with one-fiftieth in 1936.

Such giants as General Electric, General Motors, Standard Oil, United States Steel, Du Pont, employ staffs of fifty to 100 men and women. Some staffmen handle community relations; others, customer, stockholder or employee relations; some write releases and speeches; others edit house organs; still others write reports to stockholders. Some are contact men who neither write nor edit.

Most companies have a public relations staff of only half a dozen or fewer, and these men are less specialized. A small company may employ only one person, who does everything, including putting out the house organ and managing the advertising.

In recent years, public relations has been an entrance to success as administrative executive. P.R. men have risen through the ranks to become presidents of major corporations since the presidency is sometimes less an administrative than a public relations job.

Not only business companies, but also nonprofit, welfare and professional associations, trade groups, political parties, labor unions, universities, museums, hospitals, any societies or institutions that seek public support or esteem have found that they, too, require one or more full-time, professional, public relations employes. The day when untrained volunteer members were called in occasionally to do a public relations job is ended.

GOVERNMENT PUBLIC RELATIONS

One of the largest employers of public relations men and women is, not surprisingly, the Federal Government. Every bureau has them, though usually under disguised titles. Every department head, every Congressional committee, and many leading members of Congress have them too. Altogether there are 5,000 writers, editors and public relations men on the Federal payroll. While some of these jobs are civil service posts, others are "exempt," meaning that when the chief who appointed you goes out, you go out also.

The most important P.R. job in the government—and some think in the whole life of the country—is first press secretary to the President. This position and most of the other press secretaryships in the government almost invariably go to newspaper reporters who have been covering the official who appoints them.

The career of James C. Hagerty is an interesting example of the process. He was covering the New York State Legislature as a reporter for *The New York Times* when Thomas E. Dewey was elected governor in 1942. Dewey made him his executive aide. When Dwight D. Eisenhower was elected President in 1952, Dewey "gave" Hagerty to him as first press secretary. When President Eisenhower retired in 1961 and the Republicans lost the White House, Hagerty left politics to become vice-president of the American Broadcasting Company in charge of news.

The United States Information Agency is an official public relations outfit, employing hundreds of people, to promote goodwill toward America abroad. It supplies articles to foster understanding of American life and policies to newspapers and magazines all over the world. Ten newspaper columns are transmitted daily by radio to five major areas of the earth in the several languages. The U.S.I.A. produces four magazines in Washington, more than 140 others in twenty-five languages at stations overseas. The Voice of America broadcasts by radio around the world around the clock, with TV service to eighty countries.

The material supplied to newspapers and broadcasting stations is not news like that provided by the wire services, but texts of official speeches and feature stories to appeal to the countries receiving them. For example, if an Italian ski champion wins an international race at Sun Valley, the Voice of America may tape an interview with him in Italian and broadcast it to Italy.

U.S.I.A. jobs are civil service. All require a working command of a foreign language as well as ability to write. Many posts are overseas. Requirements and notices of competitive examinations may be obtained from the agency, 1776 Pennsylvania Avenue, N.W., Washington, D.C.

PUBLIC RELATIONS AGENCIES

In the major cities of the country are approximately 1,500 firms, many headed by one-time newspapermen, of public relations counselors. They are retained to represent companies, organizations and individuals. About 800 of these have headquarters or branch offices in New York City.

The leading agencies, such as Carl Byoir & Associates or Hill and Knowlton, employ large, highly paid staffs. Some others, like Batten, Barton, Durstine & Osborn, J. Walter Thompson, or N. W. Ayer, double as advertising agencies, maintaining separate divisions for the two services. Agencies such as these represent some of the biggest corporations in the world.

There is no conflict with the corporations' own P.R. staffs. Sometimes there is an arrangement for the corporation's staff to handle internal P.R., while the agency does external P.R. In other cases, the corporation's staff handles regular P.R., while the agency concentrates on a particular campaign only.

Work for an agency affords an employe broader experience than work for a single company. Promotion and pay increases are likely to be rapid. Agency employment is volatile, however, as staffs are augmented or cut according to whether accounts are gained or lost.

WHAT IT TAKES TO SUCCEED

What does it take to make a success in P.R.? Those who have achieved it seem to agree that it requires everything demanded of a good newspaperman plus two essential talents: imagination to create news and the salesmanship to sell it to client and media. In a large agency, those two talents alone are enough. Plenty of newspapermen can be hired to write releases, but there are few with salable ideas.

Competence in speaking, as well as writing, is an asset. Those who look forward to an executive career must develop a diplomatic manner, have planning skill and qualities of leadership.

Since the richest rewards lie in industrial public relations, potential beginners should acquire a business background in education and newspaper experience, advises Thomas J. Deegan, Jr., one of the leading specialists in that field.

"You should be aware of public events in the economic field, the stock market, business conditions, foreign trade, national and international politics as it affects commerce and industry," he says. "You ought to keep up with news of government agencies like the Federal Trade Commission, Securities and Exchange Commission; what the Administration's attitude toward business is. You should inform yourself of who's who and what's what in business and industry, just as kids memorize the names and batting averages of leading baseball players.

"You must read *The New York Times* and *Wall Street Journal* thoroughly every day, *Time* magazine every week, plus all the other business and economic journals you have time for.

"Without this knowledge, you can't tell what statements to make or when to make them. Besides, businessmen are coming to rely on public relations men to advise them on public, stockholder or employe reaction to any contemplated move.

"You need all the skills of the newspaperman, plus creative ideas, a critical sense of timing, a prescience of public reaction. Perhaps one must be born with all this. I don't know."

To set up your own P.R. firm takes even more than that: experience, business acumen, plenty of contacts, capital, luck.

Deegan's own career is an illustration of a success in the field. He began with six years as a financial reporter on *The New York Times* before entering public relations. World War II soon interrupted his career, but he kept his hand in as an Army public relations officer. After discharge, he became public relations director for American Airlines, then for the Chesapeake & Ohio Railway. By 1949, he was vice-president of the railway. Later he became vice-president of the Alleghany Corporation, director of Briggs Manufacturing Company, and a bank director, as well as head of the agency under his name.

Among other activities, Deegan directed Robert R. Young's dramatic proxy fight for control of the New York Central Railroad and was in charge of public relations for the New York World's Fair in 1964.

WOMEN IN P.R.

Public relations is hospitable to women.

A woman with talent can rise quickly, especially in the entertainment and cultural fields, the restaurant, food, hotel and transportation industries, in fashions, cosmetics, home furnishings and retail merchandising, in association and institutional public relations.

"Although salaries have been somewhat less than for men, top managerial positions with appropriate compensation are open to and frequently held by women," says Thomas F. Robertson, president of the Public Relations Society of America and public relations director for Eastman Kodak Company.

Unabashed by rough, male competition, women have started their own public relations counseling agencies, and some have scored notable success. Florence Herz Stone has been running her own firm in Indianapolis for twenty years. Virginia L.

Brueck's "The Write Place" in Baton Rouge, La., handles all sorts of business, though specializing in banks.

ADVANTAGES OF PUBLIC RELATIONS

"Public relations is stimulating and challenging to those who enjoy working with new ideas and coping with novel situations," says a spokesman for the Public Relations Society of America. "Many derive satisfaction from participating in a new, developing field, which significantly affects the world in which we live.

"The work can provide an enjoyable balance between desk work and face-to-face contact with others. While it provides an outlet for creative imagination and self-expression, it also offers administrative opportunity and challenge in practical action. The payoff of successful programs or campaigns . . . is exhilarating and the satisfaction of influencing others highly gratifying.

"The public relations man is not buried in his organization; he frequently has access to persons of power and influence outside. Contact with public personalities, frequent travel and speaking engagements are attractive features of the work."

The last point is particularly applicable to public relations work for public officials. The press secretary can be more than a mere press agent. He can become one of the makers of policy, though always acting behind the scenes, and thus be able to nudge history in the direction in which he believes it should move. White House correspondents say they can sometimes detect the influence of a press aide in actions even of a President.

PAY IN PUBLIC RELATIONS

The major attraction in public relations undoubtedly is the high pay compared to that in journalism in general and in newspapers in particular.

The Newspaper Fund reported that the beginning wage of the 1965 journalism graduates who went into P.R. averaged $105.63 a week, which was $9.89 more than that of beginners on daily newspapers.

Advancement in P.R. is comparatively rapid.

"A trainee in public relations for business or industry may begin at $5,000 and in a few years work up to $8,000 to $10,000," says the Public Relations Society of America. "A director of public relations for a small to medium-size company may earn $12,000 to $15,000, for a large corporation, $15,000 to $25,000. Salaries from $25,000 to $50,000 are earned by seasoned public relations executives.

"Workers in the nonprofit field [publicity for associations and institutions] are paid less . . . and there is limited opportunity to climb higher than $15,000 to $20,000."

P.R. salaries in general are highest in the biggest cities, especially New York and Chicago.

"REFUGEES FROM THE NEWSROOM"

In the course of his career, almost every big city newspaperman receives offers of public relations jobs at much higher pay than what he is getting. Many of those who switch from news work to public relations soon triple their income, according to a survey by Richard H. Costa, assistant professor at Syracuse University.

Here is his composite portrait of a "refugee from the newsroom" in public relations:

"A college graduate with a journalism major, he left a medium-incentive job as a newspaper reporter . . . earning $4,500 a year. When he decided to leave, the newspaper made little effort to keep him. He now earns $16,400 annually, finds his work more satisfying. . . ."

Professor Costa thinks the $16,400 average salary a conservative estimate. Twenty of 60 P.R. men he queried were earning over $20,000 a year, six from $18,000 to $20,000; 14 from $15,000 to $18,000; 24 from $10,000 to $15,000; only four from $7,500 to $10,000.

No random sampling of newspapermen would show two-thirds of them earning $300 a week and more.

DISADVANTAGES OF P.R.

Nevertheless, it is astonishing how many newspapermen would rather fight than switch, even for triple their pay. Some newsmen value above anything else their intellectual independence, their right to seek and state the whole truth, and the public trust in their objectivity.

This does not mean that the public relations man must lie or deceive the public. It does mean that he, like a lawyer, is an advocate, a special pleader, a counsel, a spokesman for his client.

To make the contrast clear by one actual example: When the Surgeon General of the United States warned recently against cigaret smoking as a cause of lung cancer, the stories written by newspaper reporters were very different from the news releases sent out by press agents for the tobacco industry. The reporters gave both sides of the argument; the P.R. men, one side.

Of course, if you can be press agent only for something you approve with all your heart, say the United Nations International Children's Emergency Fund, you have no problem. But most P.R. men have to take almost whatever business comes down the pike, and dedicating your life to promoting something harmful or merely trivial will not make you proud and happy.

It has been pointed out that a P.R. man may often have to "sell" his story to a reporter, editor, or both. Now, many newsmen have no talent at salesmanship; they hate the very idea of selling anything, no matter how worthy, and entered journalism to avoid huckstering.

A cub reporter for a metropolitan newspaper worked under a night city editor who ran the newsroom like Captain Bligh. A short time later, the editor resigned for a high-paying publicity job. On a minor night assignment soon afterward, the reporter found himself besought by his former tyrant to give a story favorable treatment. It was embarrassing to both.

While some publicity jobs do provide an exciting life, few offer the variety of experiences and contacts enjoyed by hundreds of reporters—though the job of press secretary to an active public official or to an extraordinary agency like the National Aeronautics and Space Administration is an exception to this rule.

By "jumping the fence" into public relations, you sacrifice some ego satisfactions of news work. You give up the by-line, the on-camera appearance; you work anonymously, offstage, in your client's name, not your own. There is a loss of status, too. The newspaperman generally enjoys more prestige and special privilege than the press agent.

Even those who go into publicity work as a first choice may find disappointment, warns Mr. Robertson.

"First, some may be disappointed to learn that the 'glamor' of public relations has been overstressed. Contrary to popular opinion, the practitioner is not involved in a continual round of cocktail parties and lunches at fashionable restaurants on an expense account. The average day is one of hard work with omnipresent deadlines and unforeseen tasks."

Nor is the work unmarred by irregular hours, haste and pressure.

"Not infrequently, public relations programs operate against deadlines with pressures characteristic of any campaign," the Public Relations Society of America says. "Under such conditions, 9 to 5 schedules go out the window. While the public relations executive will not be tied to a desk for long periods, meetings, community functions, business lunches, travel assignments, special speaking and writing commitments, unscheduled work on crises often mean longer hours for him. . . ."

Finally, there are frustrations, as in any business. The campaign you work on so hard may have disappointing results; or while it seemed successful to you, your employer or client was dissatisfied. Some clients seem to think the press agent should get a bare-faced puff into the news columns.

In the words of the Public Relations Society: "It is often difficult to measure the results of performance, and therefore to sell the worth of public relations programs."

PREPARATIONS FOR A P.R. CAREER

Mr. Robertson gives this advice on education for P.R.:

"Most employers believe that a solid, liberal arts education offers the most valuable kind of training for a career in public relations. Courses in English, writing and literature, psychology,

sociology and marketing are advantageous. There is, too, a growing recognition of the value of formal training for public relations,
especially at the graduate level."

Dr. Ray Eldon Hiebert, chairman of the department of journalism and public relations at American University in Washington,
D.C., found in a recent survey that 280 schools, roughly 15 percent of accredited colleges and universities, offer some instruction
in public relations. At least five confer the master's degree and
twelve the bachelor's degree in public relations.

In addition to college training, the most valuable preparation
for public relations is a few years of newspaper work, particularly in the appropriate, specialized field. The big agencies generally require this for employment. The smaller agencies and
public relations departments of nonprofit institutions and some
business corporations will take beginners right out of college.

FOR MORE INFORMATION

Pi Alpha Mu. National publishing, advertising and public relations
    society for men and women, undergraduate and professional.
    National offices, University of Tulsa, Tulsa 4, Okla.
Public Relations Society of America, 845 Third Avenue, New York,
    N.Y. Career Guidance Department.
United States Information Agency, 1776 Pennsylvania Avenue, N.W.,
    Washington 25, D.C. Concerning beginner's jobs, after gradua-
    tion, with Agency's press and publications service, Voice of
    America, and Foreign Service, all overseas.

BOOKLETS, PAMPHLETS

Advertising and Public Relations Training Program. General Electric
    Company, Schenectady 5, N.Y. Free.
An Occupational Guide to Public Relations. Public Relations Society of
    America, 845 Third Avenue, New York, N.Y. Free.
Angel, Juvenal L. *Careers in Public Relations.* World Trade Academy
    Press, 50 East 42nd St., New York 17, N.Y. $1.25
Careers in Publicity. No. 186. Career Research Monographs, Institute
    for Research, 537 South Dearborn, Chicago 5, Ill. $1
Public Relations Man. B-4R. Careers, Largo, Fla., 25¢

PERIODICALS

Public Relations Journal. Monthly. 845 Third Avenue, New York, N.Y.
Public Relations News. Weekly. 127 East 80th St., New York, N.Y.
Public Relations Quarterly. 305 East 45th St., New York, N.Y.
Public Relations Review. Monthly. Honolulu, Hawaii.
P.R. Reporter. Weekly. Meriden, N.H.
"Public Relations Today," *Business Week,* July 2, 1960 (14 pp.)
Quarterly Review of Public Relations. Springfield, Va.

Free-lancing, that's the life! Writing what you please, when and where it pleases you. No boss, no commuting, no regulated hours, no office routine or stupid assignments. You can live in Papeete, San Miguel Allende, Corfu, anywhere and make your living with your trusty portable.

We are sorry to wake you out of that lovely dream, but you should be told that in reality free-lancing is rarely like that. It is the hardest way to make a living in journalism. The full-time free lance needs more talent than most employed writers, more ideas, initiative and energy, iron self-discipline and lots of guts.

An independent income would help, too. It has been estimated that only three hundred nonfiction writers in the United States make a living by full-time free-lancing.

FREEDOM

And even they are "free" only in that they are not on a regular payroll. They all have a connection with one or a few magazines or syndicates that buy their work regularly and give them assignments. Many find it necessary to augment their income by "ghosting" articles and books for celebrities, writing brochures for industrial concerns or speeches for political candidates, or by occasional public relations work.

Corey Ford, humorist and free lance, expressed it in a legend on his business card: "All Kinds of Writing Done Neat and Quick."

No free lance can be certain that everything he writes will be sold. Even if there is an editor now who is buying his entire output, that source of all blessings may die, lose his job, or simply transfer his favor to another author.

GETTING THE ASSIGNMENT

Authors of fiction may write as they please, but free-lance journalists write as an editor pleases. Ninety percent of all published, nonfiction, magazine articles are assigned. Complete, unsolicited manuscripts, called "slush" in the trade, are returned unread or get a perfunctory scanning by all except a very few periodicals.

In more than half of all assignments, it is the editor who has called the writer to propose the idea. Obviously, those whom he calls are established writers.

If you, as a free lance propose the article, the standard opening procedure is to submit a query. If the editor is interested in the idea, he may ask for an outline. If the outline is rejected, the editor will not pay for your time or expenses in research and writing the outline.

If he gives you a "go ahead," you have an assignment "on spec" (speculation), meaning that he has the right to reject the finished article for any reason without paying you anything. You are then free to peddle the article to another magazine, but articles are usually so custom-made for a particular periodical that rejects are not easily sold elsewhere.

Even established writers, working on assignment for a friendly editor, get rejections once in a while. John D. Radcliffe, whose science articles appear in *Reader's Digest, Saturday Evening Post, McCall's,* and other top magazines, confesses that after twenty-five years of successful free-lancing he still has an occasional failure.

Such well-known authors are ordinarily paid their expenses and a guarantee of about 30 percent of the full fee. But that is insufficient compensation for a month's work.

Free-lance journalists work harder for themselves than staff men do for an employer. The moment the free lance stops working, he stops earning. He has no sick leave, paid vacation or pension.

As for living in Shangri-La with a portable typewriter and an adoring native girl, how many articles do you think you can think up and place from there?

To sell enough nonfiction, you must remain in close touch with the marketplace and in frequent contact with editors. You must keep yourself available for assignments. You must be familiar with topics and personalities of the moment. For that reason, many free-lance writers live in the suburbs or exurbs of New York, where most big magazines and book publishers have offices.

Keeping busy, but not too busy is a problem. It always seems there is either no work at all or more than you can handle at once. You may have to turn down a better assignment because of a prior, lower-paying commitment. An editor who is turned down a few times will stop calling.

Working on your own time is not to be equated with working at leisure. The common deadline for a 2,000- to 4,000-word magazine article is two to four weeks from "go ahead" to delivered script. In that time, you cannot make the contacts, do the necessary traveling, interviewing, research and writing of an article on an unfamiliar subject and still hold to an office employe's 5-day, 35-hour week. To meet a deadline, a free lance may have to drive himself ten hours a day for weeks. During such an emergency, some refuse to see a single friend or even answer the telephone. The deadline must not be missed, or the editor will never trust the writer again.

Between assignments, the professional free lance may rest. But not too long. He had better get busy looking for ideas and sending out queries. It is dismaying how fast an editor forgets a writer who stays out of touch.

PART-TIME FREE-LANCING

Free-lancing in one's spare time, while holding a regular job, is entirely feasible for the journalist. Most newspapermen do more or less of it, and quite a few magazine and broadcast journalists do too.

Some publishers insist that their staff members write for them exclusively. But most do not disapprove of outside writing as long as it does not benefit a competing publication or interfere with the staff job.

Indeed, there is a trend to encouraging outside free-lancing on the ground that everything that builds the journalist's reputation also benefits his full-time employer. The *Washington Star, New York Herald Tribune,* the Hearst papers are among newspapers that boast in advertisements of the books their staff newsmen have written.

Some free-lance assignments come to the newsman without his seeking.

A reporter who covers the chamber of commerce meetings may be asked to put out the chamber's yearbook. Hospitals and philanthropic societies often ask newspapermen to write their newsletters, reports, fund-raising booklets and publicity releases—sometimes on a regular basis.

It is standard procedure for a newspaper's weekend supplement to depend largely on the daily news staff for articles. When an analysis is wanted, the reporter who has been covering the news story every day is naturally asked to write it. A copyreader who visits an interesting place on his vacation may be asked to bring back a piece about it for the Sunday travel section. Fees for Sunday supplement articles, except in the syndicated magazines distributed with Sunday newspapers, are notoriously low, but the extra work is not arduous for a writer who has been living with the story daily.

When a striking feature story appears in a newspaper, the reporter may be solicited by an outside magazine to do a deeper article on the subject. Reporters covering controversial news stories are invited to appear on television or radio "meet the press" programs.

All books are written free-lance. Like magazine articles, they are done on assignment and, more often than not, proposed by the publisher. Publishers peruse the newspapers carefully for ideas, and are particularly solicitous of foreign and Washington correspondents.

It is amazing what richly laden stalks spring up sometimes from a handful of beans. From a series of three news features for *The New York Times* on the rehabilitation of juvenile delinquents, an idea for a book was extracted. The book publisher passed on the idea to *Life* magazine, which asked for two articles from the material. When the articles appeared, film rights were sold. When the hardcover book was published, the American and foreign paperback reprint rights were sold. The foreign serial rights were also sold to an English weekly paper. A few radio and television appearances and requests for similar magazine articles followed. Magic beans, indeed, picked up in the course of a reporter's daily work!

LITERARY AGENTS

Most writers who do much free-lancing have literary agents who market their work, dicker over pay, negotiate contracts. Standard commission is 10 percent of the writer's payment, with no fee for no sale.

Do you need an agent? Is he worth his fee? After twenty years of dealing through agents, we are convinced they return to the author many times their cost.

In the first place, merely being represented by an agent gives you prestige and often brings a higher price. One magazine editor, when asked for his rates, replied frankly: "That depends on who and how tough your agent is." On another sale, we received twice as much through our agent as had been offered without her.

Secondly, agents have contacts with publishers and editors which you do not have. Editors often ask them to find writers for certain articles or books.

Thirdly, agents have expertise. They know of markets you never heard of. They can suggest story ideas and helpfully criticize your script. They know how much an article should fetch, what a contract should contain and omit.

The catch in all this is that the unpublished author, who needs an agent most, has difficulty in getting one. Naturally, agents will handle only those writers likely to produce salable material. The better agencies have impressive lists of clients. Until you are worth a good agent's time, you may have to go it alone.

FREE-LANCE PAY

What you get paid for free-lance writing varies enormously according to where it is published and who you are, rather than how good it is.

Features for newspapers, including their non-syndicated weekend supplements, are easiest to sell; pay is generally low, anywhere from $5 to $100 for a piece. Syndicate services pay much more for the same kind of feature, payment varying widely according to how many newspapers buy it.

In the magazine field, most of the religious and institutional nonprofit periodicals pay nothing for free-lance articles. Commercial magazines of small circulation pay as little as three cents a word; "second-class market" magazines up to ten cents a word.

National magazines of huge circulation, like the *Saturday Evening Post, Redbook,* and the Sunday newspaper supplement magazines like *This Week,* are hardest to break into because they pay the most, about $1,000 minimum for a full-length article. Top writers command five times that or more.

Reader's Digest asserts it is the best paying magazine in the world and hospitable to beginners, even amateurs. It guarantees $1,500 for a first sale to an unknown; its "going" rate to known writers is twice that, and its maximum, limitless. The *Digest* also pays $500 or more for reprint rights to articles first published elsewhere.

Big magazines sometimes add a generous bonus, say $500, when an article turns out better than they expected or the writer was pressed for time.

First-class, and some second-class, magazines will pay a writer's expenses in gathering material. These can be heavy. *Reader's Digest* financed Cornelius Ryan's *The Longest Day,* keeping him and fourteen researchers in Europe for months; also several of John Gunther's *Inside* books, and two of James Michener's; all of these were digested in the magazine.

The New Yorker supported Lillian Ross and her family in Hollywood for a year to do her series about the making of a movie.

When you get into the Big Time, you probably will have an

agent to negotiate the fee and expense allowance. Whenever you are handling a magazine sale yourself, get a letter from the editor promising to pay a specified fee for a satisfactory script.

In the sale of books, the usual arrangement for the author is a contract with an advance payment against anticipated royalties. Try for it with an outline and sample chapter of the book. You may, however, have to submit the complete text on speculation.

Advance payments on books, if any, vary from about $500 to astronomical sums paid to Great Names. Royalties also vary according to who you are; the most common rate is 10 percent of retail sales.

One best-seller may make an author independent. On the other hand, many first books do not earn $1,000 for the writer, hardly adequate for 60,000 words that may have taken a year's work.

Development of the paperback book in recent years has brought authors more money. Though royalty rates are fractional, paperback editions run from 100,000 to millions. Books reprinted in paperback usually amass more royalties than in the original hardcover editions, but the reprint royalties usually must be split between author and original publisher.

Film rights to books are highly paid for, anywhere from $10,000 to half a million. But only a small number of the 10,000 books published annually in the United States are sold to the movies.

If and when you confront problems of reprint and movie rights, you will either know all about them or have an agent to handle them for you.

FOR MORE INFORMATION

BOOKLETS, PAMPHLETS

Professional Writing as a Career. No. 167. Institute for Research, 537 South Dearborn, Chicago 5, Ill. $1

Writer. B-7R. Careers, Largo, Fla. 25¢

PERIODICALS

The Writer. Monthly. 8 Arlington St., Boston, Mass. 40¢ copy, $5 a year.

Writer's Digest. Monthly. 22 East 12th St., Cincinnati, Ohio. $4 a year.

MARKET GUIDE BOOKS

Literary Market Place. R. R. Bowker Company, 1180 Avenue of the Americas, New York, N.Y. $7.45. Lists magazines, book publishers, play and television producers, agents, etc.

The Writer's Handbook. 8 Arlington St., Boston, Mass. $6.95. Advice and 2,000 places to sell articles and books, etc.

Writer's Market. 22 East 12th St., Cincinnati, Ohio. $5.95. 4,000 places to sell writing.

Writer's Yearbook. 8 Arlington St., Boston, Mass. Volume of advice.

5

HOW TO GO ABOUT IT

Chapter
Twenty-two | **GETTING STARTED**
| **IN JOURNALISM**

Finding that first job in journalism is no problem, as we have said, for journalism school graduates or other college graduates with some experience or contacts in the field. But how do you go about it if you have not had those head starts?

In the first place, you may have to resign yourself to beginning on a small daily or weekly newspaper, a small or middle-size broadcasting station, on a second-rank magazine, on a business-paper or house organ, or on the public relations staff of a small agency, business concern or nonprofit institution.

If you choose the daily newspaper and broadcasting fields, you probably will have to go out of New York, Washington, Chicago, Los Angeles, and the other big cities, though not out of their suburbs, for that first job. If you pick magazines or public relations, on the other hand, you will find more job opportunities in New York than in all the rest of the country combined.

With that settled, how do you locate an opening? Here are some sources of job information.

PLACEMENT OFFICES

Your college placement office may have some calls for journalism personnel even though the college gives no journalism courses. Worth checking too are the placement bureaus of the organizations listed in this book.

"HELP WANTED" ADS

On a recent Sunday, we counted 153 advertisements for writers or editors of newspapers and magazines of all kinds and for public relations people in *The New York Times,* largest compendium of such notices in the world.

Most of the employing companies were in New York and its suburbs. The rest were in New Jersey, Connecticut, a few in upstate New York, the Midwest, and California.

Editor and Publisher, weekly magazine of the newspaper industry, carries in each issue thirty to fifty ads for reporters and editors, not only on newspapers, but also on magazines and house organs, and for public relations personnel.

The *Publisher's Auxiliary,* trade paper of community newspapers, carries many help wanted ads for beginners on good weeklies in each issue.

The *Quill,* magazine of Sigma Delta Chi, professional journalists' fraternity, and the *Iowa Publisher,* magazine of the Iowa State University School of Journalism, put out "career issues" that contain many display ads by newspapers and broadcasting stations for newsmen, mostly in the interior of the country.

EMPLOYMENT AGENCIES

In New York and some other big cities, there are employment agencies specializing in jobs for journalists. Their ads appear in the classified sections of newspapers.

Edward J. Farley of Headline Personnel in New York says that his agency gets 1,200 requests annually from newspapers mostly in the Northeast and Middle West; about 450 from trade papers, 200 from magazines, 300 from public relations departments and house organs. Salaries range from $50 a week for cubs on small newspapers to $20,000 and up for experienced trade paper editors and public relations men. Requests for men are three to five times as many as for women. Most editors want some experience—on a campus publication at least.

The agency has recently installed a department to answer increasing calls for broadcast personnel.

APPLYING TO THE EMPLOYER

In some ways, the simplest thing to do is apply directly to the company you would like to work for. Familiarizing yourself with the publication would seem an obvious preparation, yet many applicants neglect it. If you apply for a job on a paper you have never bothered to read, your ignorance will be revealed in your first interview by the editor.

The best introduction to an editor is through someone who knows him, perhaps an advertiser or one of your instructors. If you can't find anyone to intercede for you, write him a letter yourself.

On a newspaper, apply to the city editor. His name is found in N. W. Ayer's *Directory of Newspapers and Periodicals* or in *Editor and Publisher Yearbook,* both of which are kept in any large reference library.

On a magazine, address the managing editor, whose name is on the masthead. In a broadcasting station, the man to see is the news director; in a business concern or institution it is the public relations director. These names can be obtained by telephoning the personnel departments. In any case, never make a job application not addressed to someone by name. A good reporter will get the name.

Then type *perfectly* a brief letter requesting an interview to apply for a job—personal printed stationery is a small, worthwhile investment—and attach a résumé of your qualifications.

Some applicants go to the expense of having résumés reproduced in photo-offset and enclosed in manuscript covers, but a couple of neatly typed, white sheets, 8½ by 11 inches, stapled together will do.

The résumé should state your name, age, address and telephone number (both at school and at home); what job you are seeking and the date you can start; your high school and college education, your major and principal minor subjects, any specialties that might equip you for the job.

Be sure to mention any journalistic experience, professional or amateur, any honors or prizes in writing, any work in college dramatics or debating if you are applying for broadcasting work. State whether you have any special skills like shorthand or whether you speak a foreign language. You should also tell what you hope to specialize in eventually.

Attach a photograph, and copies of any recommendations from instructors or previous employers.

The Magazine World by Professor Roland E. Wolseley discusses résumés in detail with illustrations of attractive formats.

It is not only beginners, but also young journalists of some experience, who submit résumés of their qualifications when applying for jobs.

THE INTERVIEW

You will be surprised at how many favorable replies you get. You may even get a call a year or two later, long after you have another job. Even if they have no opening at the moment, editors keep every possible application on file.

You do not need to be told to dress conservatively for the interview and to behave in a business-like manner. Speak right up, but do not pitch a hard sell or turn on an artificial charm.

Have any clippings of your stories, certificates of awards, prizes, letters of recommendation with you. An attractive way to show them is in transparent sleeves clipped into a loose-leaf, ring binder.

Be prepared to discuss questions like these:

Why do you want to go into journalism?

What would you like to do for us?

What are you most interested in?

How would you improve our publication?

The interviewer may slant the discussion to test your general knowledge of the field and his publication in particular. While you are not required to be an expert, you are expected to be well-informed.

More and more employers are giving aptitude tests to applicants. Do not be surprised if an editor hands you a sheet of facts and asks you to sit down and bat out a news story then and there. He may ask you to write an autobiographical sketch or a short feature about anything you wish. He may send you out on an actual assignment that very day, or he may give you a piece of copy to edit or rewrite at once.

One final tip: make your enthusiasm evident. But don't fake it. If you don't feel it, go elsewhere.

Chapter Twenty-three

GETTING AHEAD
IN JOURNALISM

Getting a first spot in journalism is not so difficult as finding a place with a future that is right for you.

The first job—indeed, the first three jobs—may not be it.

"My students go out to their first jobs full of enthusiasm," says Professor Penn T. Kimball of the Columbia School of Journalism. "A year or so later, they write me of their disappointment. They say their assignments are dull or trivial, their good ideas rejected, or their publisher won't permit them to undertake a public service story they want to do."

The only solution to such a situation is to move, and keep moving if you have to, while you are still young, before you have to support a family and before you acquire too much in the job to give up. We have known many reporters who resigned in despair or even were fired, but who immediately afterward scored notable successes elsewhere.

All companies prefer to hire young people; some will not employ anyone on the lower echelons over the age of thirty. If you have not made a success by forty, you probably are never going to make it in these frenetic days.

Your first job may be low man on a local paper. Don't despair. The important thing is to gain experience that will help you get a better job. If you are good, you'll get it.

A young man of our acquaintance accepted a cub's beat on a small New Jersey paper when he graduated from a liberal arts college three years ago. After two and one-half years learning the journalistic ropes, he applied to one of Long Island's lively suburban papers. He is employed there now, writing "in-depth" reports on community problems.

"He'll stay with us about three years," predicts his editor, "and then he'll move on again to a still better job on a still bigger paper."

Few leading journalists have had an Horatio Alger career of office boy to president in one company.

Turner Catledge, executive editor of *The New York Times*, began as a cub on the *Neshoba* (Mississippi) *Democrat* and tore through six papers in eight years before making the reportorial staff of *The Times*. Even after that, he left for a few years on the *Chicago Sun* before returning to a better job on *The Times*.

Herbert R. Mayes, one of America's most important magazine editors, began as editor of the *Inland Merchant*, which had a circulation of 4,000 among small-town grocers. He served as editor of three small businesspapers before he got a foothold on a national consumer magazine.

You will be able to tell quickly whether a job is wrong for you. You will *feel* it.

FULL SPEED AHEAD

Once you get on the right track in an organization where you love the work and the boss loves you, you can move ahead faster than ever before in journalism.

Joseph L. Oppenheimer, thirty-seven-year-old editor of the *Outlook*, an important financial news journal, recently made an informal survey of the rate of advancement in all areas of journalism. Here is his conclusion:

"Few other businesses, professions or industries afford equal opportunities for advancement. Many of the nation's top newspaper, magazine, radio and television jobs are held by young men under forty or were acquired by them before they reached forty."

"A youngster today can accomplish in two or three years what formerly took ten years," another leading editor said, "if he shows the talent."

HOW THEY MOVED AHEAD

Talent, however great, must be pushed into the light. Few editors have the time to beat the bushes to discover hidden genius, and some are too indifferent or blind to recognize it when they do see it. Talent must be thrust upon their notice, again and again, before it is rewarded.

"You have to prove yourself to your superiors before you get the assignments you think you should get," warns Miles H. Wolff, editor of the *Greensboro Daily News* and past president of the American Society of Newspaper Editors. "It is rare that they fall into your lap."

Editor Wolff likes to recall two eager trainees who came to him during their college vacation.

"They were given the usual routine assignments, but they weren't satisfied. When a seeing-eye dog saved his master's life and was killed, they worked up a follow story on their own volition. They found out how much it would cost the blind man to get another seeing-eye dog and what he was doing now that he had no guide. They weren't satisfied to be routine reporters, and they quickly made a niche for themselves on the city staff."

Rene J. Cappon, forty-year-old managing editor of the A.P., recalls how he wrote his way out of a dull desk job on the agency's Kansas City Bureau by coming up frequently with features on his own initiative.

"Drive" is the word for Fred W. Friendly, former president of CBS News. He began in broadcasting in 1938 with "Footprints in the Sands of Time," a radio series of five-minute, dramatic biographies of founders of American industries. He wrote, produced, narrated them all himself and sold them to a Providence, Rhode Island, station for $5 each.

PLAN TO STAY

If you become a reporter, you are sure to be told by many of the men you interview, "You know, I used to be a newspaperman myself once."

It is a remarkable fact that many business and professional

men, right up to the heads of big companies and important public officials, did indeed give journalism a brief whirl in their youth. However, most of them—with some distinguished exceptions— were no great shakes at it. Generally speaking, the best journalists stick to journalism.

We wish you would not go into journalism as a youthful escapade, like going to sea for a while, before settling down. Journalism is worthy to be practiced as a lifelong occupation by mature men and women. It can even be performed as a mission for the highest purposes.

Is it the mission for you? If, after reading this book, the answer is no, all right; we are glad to have saved you from a misstep. If the answer is yes, go to it. The country and all mankind need good journalists. Now, as never before!

APPENDIX
and
BIBLIOGRAPHY

Schools and Courses in Journalism

Courses in journalism, in one form or another, are offered in several hundred colleges in the United States. The establishment varies from large, specialized schools with their own faculties to a single course given by one instructor within the English department.

Listed below are 150 institutions that maintain separate schools or departments of journalism with provision for majoring in the subject. Degrees in journalism conferred, if any, are noted for each institution.

For each school, also, the "sequences," or groups of journalism courses given, are listed. The sequences accredited by the American Council on Education for Journalism as meeting its standards of scope and teaching are printed in *italics*. The forty-seven institutions that have won accreditation in one or more sequences are marked by an asterisk. Lack of accreditation, however, is not necessarily a reflection on the quality of the institution, since some have not sought approval by the ACEJ.

More information is contained in *The Journalism Educator*, Directory Issue, published annually by the American Society of Journalism School Administrators at Duquesne University, Pittsburgh, Pa., at $2. The student is also advised to write for specific information directly to the institution he is particularly interested in.

Alabama

University of Alabama, Tuscaloosa.
  Journalism Department.
  News, Industrial Editing, Public
    Relations, Advertising.
  Degrees: bachelor's, master's.
Howard College, Birmingham.
  Journalism Department.
  News-Editorial.
  Degree: bachelor's.

Arizona

Arizona State University, Tempe.
  Mass Communications Depart-
    ment.
  News-Editorial, Radio-Television.
  Degree: bachelor's.
°University of Arizona, Tucson.
  Department of Journalism.
  News-Editorial.
  Degree: bachelor's.

Arkansas

Arkansas State College, Jonesboro
  Journalism Department.
  Journalism, Printing, Radio.
  Degree: bachelor's.
University of Arkansas, Fayetteville.
  Journalism Department.
  Degree: bachelor's.

California

California State College, Long
    Beach.
  Journalism Department.
  News Writing, Newspaper Pro-
    duction, Yearbook Produc-
    tion, School Journalism, Pub-
    lic Relations.
California State Polytechnic College,
    San Luis Obispo.
  Journalism Department.
  Agricultural, Home Economics,
    Business and Industrial,
    Community Journalism.
  Degree: bachelor's.
University of California, Berkeley.
  Journalism Department.
  News-Editorial, Communications
    Research, Urban and En-

vironment Criticism, Interna-
    tional Persuasion.
University of California, Los
    Angeles.
  Journalism Department.
  News-Editorial.
  Degree: master's only.
°Fresno State College, Fresno.
  Journalism Department.
  News-Editorial, Technical Jour-
    nalism, Radio and Television
    News Communication, Public
    Relations, Advertising.
  Degree: bachelor's.
Los Angeles State College, Los
    Angeles.
  Journalism Department.
  News-Editorial.
Orange State College, Fullerton.
  Journalism Department.
  News-Editorial.
Sacramento State College,
    Sacramento.
  Journalism Department.
  General Journalism.
  Degree: bachelor's.
San Diego State College, San Diego.
  Journalism Department.
  News, Industrial Journalism,
    Radio-Television.
  Degree: bachelor's.
San Fernando Valley State College,
    Northridge.
  Journalism Department.
  News.
  Degree: bachelor's.
San Francisco State College, San
    Francisco.
  Journalism Department.
  News-Editorial, General Sec-
    ondary School Credential,
    English Language Arts with
    journalism emphasis.
  Degree: bachelor's.
°San José State College, San José.
  Department of Journalism and
    Advertising.
  News-Editorial, Public Relations,

Advertising, Photo-Journalism, Radio-Television, Professional Writing.
Degree: bachelor's.
University of Southern California,
Los Angeles.
School of Journalism.
News-Editorial, Public Relations.
Degree: bachelor's.
°Stanford University, Palo Alto.
Department of Communication
and Journalism.
News-Editorial.
Degree: bachelor's, master's.

Colorado
Colorado State University, Fort
Collins.
Technical Journalism Division,
Department of English.
Technical Journalism.
Degree: bachelor's.
°University of Colorado, Boulder.
School of Journalism.
News-Editorial, Advertising,
Radio-Television.
Degree: bachelor's.
University of Denver, Denver.
Journalism Department.
News-Editorial.
Degree: bachelor's.

Connecticut
University of Bridgeport, Bridgeport.
Journalism Department.
News-Editorial, Industrial Journalism, Advertising.
Degree: bachelor's.
University of Connecticut, Storrs.
Journalism Department.
News.

District of Columbia
American University, Washington.
Journalism Department.
News-Editorial, Radio-Television,
Public Relations.
Degrees: bachelor's, master's.
George Washington University,
Washington.

Journalism Department.
News-Editorial.
Degree: bachelor's.
Florida
Florida Southern College, Lakeland.
Journalism Department.
News, Public Relations,
Advertising.
Degree: bachelor's.
°University of Florida, Gainesville.
School of Journalism and Communication.
*Editorial-News, General Radio
and Television, Public Relations, Advertising.*
Degrees: bachelor's, master's.
University of Miami, Coral Gables.
Journalism Department.
News-Editorial.
Degree: bachelor's.
Georgia
Georgia State College, Atlanta.
Journalism Department.
News-Editorial.
°University of Georgia, Athens.
Henry W. Grady School of
Journalism.
*News-Editorial, Broadcasting,
Public Relations, Advertising,*
Journalism-Literary Appreciation, Journalistic-Secretarial, Home Economics
Journalism.
Degrees: bachelor's, master's.
Idaho
Idaho State University, Pocatello.
Journalism Department.
News-Editorial, Media Management, Journalism-Social
Science, English-Journalism,
Journalism-Speech in Mass
Communications, Teaching
Minor in Journalism.
Degree: bachelor's.
University of Idaho, Moscow.
Journalism Department.
News.
Degree: bachelor's.

Illinois

Bradley University, Peoria.
Journalism Department.
News-Editorial, Public Relations.
Degree: bachelor's.
°University of Illinois, Urbana.
College of Journalism and
Communications.
News-Editorial, Radio-Television,
Advertising.
Degrees: bachelor's, master's,
Ph.D.
Mundelein College, Chicago.
Journalism Department.
Degree: bachelor's.
Northern Illinois University,
De Kalb.
Journalism Department.
News-Editorial, Community and
Suburban Newspapers,
Industrial Press.
Degree: bachelor's.
°Northwestern University, Evanston.
Medill School of Journalism.
News-Editorial, Radio-Television
News, Magazine, Advertising.
Degrees: bachelor's, master's,
Ph.D.
°Southern Illinois University,
Carbondale.
Journalism Department.
News-Editorial, Community
Journalism, Radio-Television
News, Magazine, *Advertising.*
Degrees: bachelor's, master's.

Indiana

Butler University, Indianapolis.
Journalism Department.
News, Radio.
Degree: bachelor's.
Depauw University, Greencastle.
Journalism Area in Department
of English.
°Indiana University, Bloomington.
Department of Journalism, De-
partment of Radio and
Television.
News-Editorial, Business Adver-

tising, *Radio and Television.*
Degrees: bachelor's, master's.
University of Notre Dame, Notre
Dame.
Journalism Department.
Degree: bachelor's.
St. Joseph's College, Rensselaer.
Journalism Department.
News.
Degree, bachelor's.
St. Mary-of-the-Woods College,
St. Mary-of-the-Woods.
Journalism Department.
Degree: bachelor's.

Iowa

Drake University, Des Moines.
School of Journalism.
News-Editorial, Radio-Television,
Magazines-Books, Photo-
Journalism, Creative Adver-
tising, General Journalism.
Degree: bachelor's.
Grinnell College, Grinnell.
Journalism Area in Division of
Language and Literature.
°Iowa State University of Agricul-
ture and Mechanic Arts,
Ames.
Department of Technical Journal-
ism.
Technical Journalism.
Degrees: bachelor's, master's.
°University of Iowa, Iowa City.
School of Journalism.
Editorial, Magazine, Radio-
Television, Public Relations,
Advertising, Community
Journalism, Mass Communi-
cations, High School Journal-
ism Teaching, Pictorial Jour-
nalism.
Degrees: bachelor's, master's.
Ph.D. in Communications
only.

Kansas

°Kansas State University of Agriculture and Applied Science,
Manhattan.

Department of Technical
Journalism.
*Agricultural, Home Economics
Journalism, News-Editorial.*
Degrees: bachelor's, master's.
°University of Kansas, Lawrence.
William Allen White School of
Journalism and Public
Information.
*News-Editorial, Radio-Television,
Advertising.*
Degrees: bachelor's, master's.
University of Wichita, Wichita.
Journalism Department.
News-Editorial, Radio-Television,
Community Journalism,
Advertising.
Degree: bachelor's.

Kentucky
°University of Kentucky, Lexington.
School of Journalism.
General Editorial, Radio, Com-
munity Journalism.
Degree: bachelor's.

Louisiana
°Louisiana State University and
Agricultural and Mechanical
College, Baton Rouge.
School of Journalism.
News-Editorial, Publishing
Management.
Degrees: bachelor's, master's.
Loyola University, New Orleans.
Journalism Department.
News Writing, Business and
Journalism, Public Relations
and Journalism.
Degree: bachelor's.
Northwestern State College of
Louisiana, Natchitoches.
Area in Department of Languages.
Degree: bachelor's.

Maryland
°University of Maryland, College
Park.
Department of Journalism.
News-Editorial, Public Relations.
Degree: bachelor's.

Massachusetts
°Boston University, Boston.
Journalism Division, School of
Public Communication.
*News-Editorial, Photo-Journalism,
Public Relations,* Magazine,
Advertising.
Degrees: bachelor's, master's.
Massachusetts University, Amherst.
Division of Journalism.
Editorial.
Degree: bachelor's.
Simmons College, Boston.
School of Publication.
Editorial, Publishing Arts,
Technical Writing.
Degree: bachelor's.

Michigan
Central Michigan University,
Mount Pleasant.
Journalism Department.
Editorial, Hign School Journalism
Teaching.
Degree: bachelor's.
Detroit University, Detroit.
Journalism Department.
News Editing.
Degree: bachelor's.
Marygrove College, Detroit.
Journalism Department.
Degree: bachelor's.
°Michigan State University, East
Lansing.
School of Journalism.
*News-Editorial, Radio-TV,
Advertising.*
Degrees: bachelor's, master's.
°University of Michigan, Ann
Arbor.
Department of Journalism.
News-Editorial, Magazine, Foreign
Correspondence, Community
Newspapers, Government
Reporting, Science Writing,
Broadcasting, Public Rela-
tions, Advertising.
Degrees: bachelor's, master's.
Wayne State University, Detroit.

Journalism Department.
Newspaper-Magazine, Television-Radio, Public Relations, Advertising.
Degree: bachelor's.

Minnesota
° University of Minnesota, Minneapolis.
School of Journalism.
News-Editorial, Advertising, Radio-Television, Magazine, Public Relations.
Degrees: bachelor's, master's. Ph.D.

Mississippi
Mississippi State College for Women, Columbus.
Journalism Department.
News-Editorial.
Degree: bachelor's.
University of Mississippi, University.
Journalism Department.
News.
Degrees: bachelor's, master's.
Southern Mississippi University, Hattiesburg.
Journalism Department.
News-Editorial.
Degree: bachelor's.

Missouri
Lincoln University, Jefferson City.
Journalism Department.
News-Editorial, Advertising-Management.
Degree: bachelor's.
° University of Missouri, Columbia.
School of Journalism.
News-Editorial, Magazine, News-paper Publishing, Photo-Journalism, Radio-Television, Advertising-Production.
Degrees: bachelor's, master's.

Montana
° Montana State University, Missoula.
School of Journalism.

News-Editorial, Radio-Television, Advertising, Community, Magazine.
Degree: bachelor's.

Nebraska
Creighton University, Omaha.
Journalism Department.
News-Editorial, Radio-Television, Advertising.
Degree: bachelor's.
° University of Nebraska, Lincoln.
School of Journalism.
News-Editorial, Radio-Television, Educational, Home Economics, Agricultural Journalism, Advertising.
Degree: bachelor's.
Municipal University of Omaha, Omaha.
Journalism Department.
News.
Degree: bachelor's.

Nevada
University of Nevada, Reno.
Journalism Department.
News-Editorial, Radio-Television, High School Teaching, Public Relations, Advertising.
Degree: bachelor's.

New Jersey
Rider College, Trenton.
Journalism Department.
News.
Degree: bachelor's.
° Rutgers State University, New Brunswick.
School of Journalism.
Editorial, Public Relations, Advertising.
Degree: bachelor's.
Seton Hall University, South Orange.
Communication Arts Department.
News-Editorial, Radio-Television.
Degree: bachelor's.

New Mexico
New Mexico Highlands University, Las Vegas.

Journalism Division.
News.
Degree: bachelor's.
New Mexico State College, Las
Cruces.
Department of Journalism.
News-Editorial.
°University of New Mexico,
Albuquerque.
Department of Journalism.
News-Editorial.
Degree: bachelor's.

New York
°Columbia University, New York.
Graduate School of Journalism.
News-Editorial.
Degree: master's only. (Limits
the number of women.)
Fordham University, New York.
Division of Journalism.
Journalism, Broadcasting.
Degree: bachelor's.
Long Island University, Brooklyn.
Journalism Department.
News, Radio-Television, Public
Relations, Magazines.
Degree: bachelor's.
New York University, New York.
Journalism Department.
Newspaper, Magazine, Business
and Industrial, Public Rela-
tions.
Degree: bachelor's.
St. Bonaventure University, St.
Bonaventure.
Journalism Department.
News-Editorial.
Degree: bachelor's.
°Syracuse University, Syracuse.
School of Journalism.
*News-Editorial, Magazine, Ad-
vertising,* Religion, Literary,
Graphic Arts Journalism,
Public Relations.
Degrees: bachelor's, master's.

North Carolina
°University of North Carolina,
Chapel Hill.

School of Journalism.
News-Editorial.
Degrees: bachelor's, master's.

North Dakota
University of North Dakota,
Grand Forks.
Journalism Department.
News-Editorial, Publishing,
Advertising.
Degree: bachelor's.

Ohio
Bowling Green State University,
Bowling Green.
School of Journalism.
News, Photo-Journalism, Publi-
cation Management, Public
Relations, Radio.
°Kent State University, Kent.
School of Journalism.
News-Editorial, Photo-Journalism,
Radio-Television, Public
Relations, option in Business
and Industrial Journalism.
Degree: bachelor's.
°Ohio State University, Columbus.
School of Journalism.
News-Editorial, Magazine,
Broadcasting, Photo-Jour-
nalism, Public Relations.
Degrees: bachelor's, master's.
°Ohio University, Athens.
School of Journalism.
*News Writing and Editing,
Radio-Television, Magazine,
Public Relations, Advertising-
Management.*
Degrees: bachelor's, master's.
Ohio Wesleyan University,
Delaware.
Journalism Department.
News-Editorial.
Degree: bachelor's.
College of Steubenville, Steuben-
ville.
Journalism Department.
News.
Degree: bachelor's.
University of Dayton, Dayton.

Communication Arts Department.
Communication Arts, Journalism,
   Broadcasting Journalism,
   Theater, Speech.
Degree: bachelor's.

Oklahoma
Central State College, Edmond.
Department of Journalism.
News-Editorial.
Oklahoma Baptist University,
   Shawnee.
Journalism Department.
Editorial, Religious Journalism,
   Photo-Journalism.
Oklahoma City University,
   Oklahoma City.
Journalism Department.
News-Editorial, Advertising.
Degree: bachelor's.
°Oklahoma State University,
   Stillwater.
School of Journalism.
*News-Editorial, Advertising-
   Management,* Agricultural,
   Broadcasting, Home Eco-
   nomics, Industrial, Com-
   munity Journalism.
Degrees: bachelor's, master's,
°University of Oklahoma, Norman.
H. H. Herbert School of Jour-
   nalism.
*General Editorial, Professional
   Writing, News-Advertising,
   Advertising-Business, Public
   Relations, Radio-Television.*
Degrees: bachelor's, master's.
University of Tulsa, Tulsa.
Journalism Department.
News-Editorial, Radio-Television
   News, Advertising.
Degree: bachelor's.

Oregon
Oregon State University, Corvallis.
Journalism Department.
°University of Oregon, Eugene.
School of Journalism.
News-Editorial, Broadcasting,
   Advertising-Management.

Degrees: bachelor's, master's.

Pennsylvania
Duquesne University, Pittsburgh.
Journalism Department.
News-Editorial, Radio-Television,
   Public Relations, Advertising.
Degree: bachelor's.
Lehigh University, Bethlehem.
Journalism Division.
News-Editorial.
Degree: bachelor's.
°Pennsylvania State University,
   University Park.
School of Journalism.
News-Editorial, Broadcasting,
   Advertising.
Degrees: bachelor's, master's.
University of Pennsylvania,
   Philadelphia.
Annenberg School of Communica-
   tions.
Temple University, Philadelphia.
Department of Communications.
Editorial-News, Radio-Television.
Degree: bachelor's.

Rhode Island
University of Rhode Island,
   Kingston.
Journalism Department.
Newspaper Reporting and
   Editing.

South Carolina
Furman University, Greenville.
Journalism Department.
News.
Degree: bachelor's.
°University of South Carolina,
   Columbia.
School of Journalism.
News-Editorial, Advertising.
Degrees: bachelor's, master's.

South Dakota
°South Dakota State College of
   Agriculture and Mechanics
   Arts, Brookings.
Department of Printing and
   Journalism.

News-Editorial, Agricultural,
Home Economics, Journal-
ism.
Degrees: bachelor's, master's.
University of South Dakota,
Vermillion.
Journalism Department.
Editorial, Radio-Television,
Advertising.
Degree: bachelor's.

Tennessee

Memphis State University, Memphis.
Journalism Department.
News, Radio-Television, Adver-
tising.
Degree: bachelor's.
*University of Tennessee, Knoxville.
School of Journalism.
News-Editorial, Radio-Television,
Advertising-Management.
Degree: bachelor's.

Texas

Abilene Christian College, Abilene.
Journalism Department.
News.
Baylor University, Waco.
Journalism Department.
News-Editorial, Religious Jour-
nalism, Photography, Public
Relations, Advertising.
Degree: bachelor's.
East Texas State College, Commerce.
Journalism Division in Depart-
ment of Communications.
News-Editorial, Photo-Journalism,
Advertising-Public Relations.
Degrees: bachelor's, master's.
University of Houston, Houston.
Department of Communication
Arts.
Magazine and Special Writing,
News-Editorial, Photo-Jour-
nalism, Radio-Television
News, Teaching of Journal-
ism in Secondary Schools,
Typography.
Degree: bachelor's.

North Texas State University,
Denton.
Department of Journalism.
News Writing-Editing, Teaching
of Journalism.
Sam Houston State Teachers
College, Huntsville.
Journalism Department.
Editorial, News, Advertising,
Public Relations, Sports.
Southern Methodist University,
Dallas.
Journalism Department.
News-Editorial, Magazine, Public
Relations, Advertising,
Teaching and Publication
Supervision.
Degree: bachelor's.
Southwest Texas State College,
San Marcos.
Journalism Department.
News-Editing.
Degree: bachelor's.
*Texas Agricultural and Mechanical
University, College Station.
Department of Journalism.
*Agricultural, Community Jour-
nalism.*
Degree: bachelor's.
Texas Christian University, Fort
Worth.
Journalism Department.
News-Editorial, Advertising.
Degree: bachelor's.
Texas Southern University, Houston.
Journalism Department.
News-Editorial, Photo-Journalism,
Advertising.
Degree: bachelor's.
Texas Technological College,
Lubbock.
Journalism Department.
News, Radio-Television, Com-
munity Journalism, Adver-
tising.
Degree: bachelor's.
*University of Texas, Austin.
School of Journalism.

*News-Editorial, Magazine Writing
and Editing, Advertising,*
Public Affairs Reporting,
Community Journalism,
Public Relations, Teaching
of Journalism, Radio-Tele-
vision News.
Degree: bachelor's.
Texas Western College, El Paso.
Journalism Department.
News, Advertising.
Degree: bachelor's.
Texas Woman's University, Denton.
Journalism Department.
News-Editorial, Advertising.
Degree: bachelor's.
Trinity University, San Antonio.
Journalism Department.
News-Editorial, Magazine Writ-
ing, Radio-News, Advertising,
Public Relations.
Degree: bachelor's.
West Texas State College, Canyon.
Department of Journalism.
News-Editorial.

Utah
Brigham Young University, Provo.
Communications Department.
News-Editorial, Radio-Television,
Journalism Education, Ad-
vertising-Public Relations.
Degrees: bachelor's, master's.
Utah State University, Logan.
Journalism Division in Depart-
ment of English.
Journalism, Writing, Mass Com-
munications.
Degree: bachelor's.
University of Utah, Salt Lake City.
Journalism Department.
News-Editorial, Radio-Television,
Journalism Education, Ad-
vertising.
Degrees: bachelor's, master's.

Virginia
*Washington and Lee University,
Lexington.

Department of Journalism and
Communications.
News-Editorial.
Degree: bachelor's.

Washington
St. Martin's College, Olympia.
Journalism Department.
Seattle University, Seattle.
Journalism Department.
News.
Degree: bachelor's.
Washington State University,
Pullman.
Department of Communications.
General Journalism, Agricultural
Journalism, Radio-Television.
Degree: bachelor's.
*University of Washington, Seattle.
School of Communications.
*News-Editorial, General Radio-
Television, Advertising.*
Degree: bachelor's.

West Virginia
Marshall University, Huntington.
Journalism Department.
News-Editorial, Advertising-
Journalism.
Degree: bachelor's.
*West Virginia University, Morgan-
town.
School of Journalism.
*News-Editorial, Advertising-
Management,* Radio-Tele-
vision, Technical Journalism,
Public Relations, Agriculture-
Science, Journalism Edu-
cation, Graduate.
Degrees: bachelor's, master's.

Wisconsin
*Marquette University, Milwaukee.
College of Journalism.
News-Editorial, Advertising,
Radio-Television.
Degrees: bachelor's, master's.
*University of Wisconsin, Madison.
School of Journalism.

News-Editorial, Advertising-Management.
Degrees: bachelor's, master's, Ph.D.
Department of Agricultural Journalism.
Agricultural, Home Economics Journalism, Science Writing, Agricultural Advertising,

Public Relations.
Degrees: bachelor's, master's.

Wyoming
University of Wyoming, Laramie.
Journalism Department.
News, Radio-Television, Public Relations, Advertising.
Degree: bachelor's.

A Selected Bibliography of Recent Books |

OTHER CAREER GUIDES

Brucker, Herbert. *The Journalist.* New York: Macmillan, 1962, $3.50.
Gemmill, Henry, and Kilgore, Bernard (eds.). *Do You Belong in Journalism?* New York: Appleton-Century-Crofts, 1959, $3.00.
Ryan, Bernard, and Ryan, Leonard. *So You Want to Go into Journalism.* New York: Harper & Row, 1962, $3.50.
Schaleben, Arville. *Your Future in Journalism.* New York: Richards Rosen Press, 1961, $2.95.
Stein, M. L. *Your Career in Journalism.* New York: Messner, 1965, $3.95.

JOURNALISM IN GENERAL

Bond, F. Fraser. *An Introduction to Journalism.* New York: Macmillan, 1961, $5.95.
Emery, Ault, and Agee. *Introduction to Mass Communications* (2nd. rev. ed). New York: Dodd, Mead, 1966.
Gerald, James E. *Social Responsibility of the Press.* Minneapolis: University of Minnesota Press, 1963, $5.00.
Hohenberg, John. *The Professional Journalist.* New York: Holt, Rinehart and Winston, 1960, $6.50.
Lacey, Dan M. *Freedom and Communications* (2nd. ed.). Urbana, Ill.: University of Illinois Press, 1965, $3.00; paper, 95¢.
Mott, Frank Luther. *American Journalism: a History 1690–1960* (3rd rev. ed.). New York: Macmillan, 1962, $8.95.
Peterson, Theodore, Jenson, Jay, and Rivers, William L. *The Mass Media and Modern Society.* New York: Holt, Rinehart and Winston, 1966, $5.75.

NEWSPAPERS

Barrett, Edward W. *Journalists in Action.* New York: Appleton-Century-Crofts, 1963, $5.95.

Botter, David. *News Reporters and What They Do*. New York: Franklin Watts, Inc., 1959, $3.95.

Casey, Ralph D. (ed.). *The Press in Perspective*. Baton Rouge: Louisiana State University Press, 1963, $6.00.

Cater, Douglass. *The Fourth Branch of Government*. Boston: Houghton Mifflin, 1959, $3.50.

Copple, Neale. *Depth Reporting*. Englewood Cliffs, N.J.: Prentice-Hall, 1963, $5.95.

Hohenberg, John. *Foreign Correspondence*. New York: Columbia University Press, 1964, $8.95.

Johnson, Stanley P., and Harriss, J. *The Complete Reporter*. New York: Macmillan, 1965, $6.95.

Liebling, A. J. *The Press*. New York: Ballantine Books, 1961, paper 95¢.

MacDougall, C. E. *Interpretive Reporting*. New York: Macmillan, 1963, $7.50.

WEEKLY NEWSPAPERS

Byerly, Kenneth R. *Community Journalism*. Philadelphia: Chilton Books, 1961, $4.97.

MAGAZINES

Mott, Frank Luther. *History of American Magazines*. Cambridge, Mass.: Harvard University Press, 1957. Vol. I, $10; Vol. II, $8.50; Vol. III, $9.00; Vol. IV, $12.50.

Peterson, Theodore. *Magazines in the Twentieth Century* (2nd rev. ed.). Urbana, Ill.: University of Illinois Press, 1964, $7.50.

Wolseley, Roland E. *Understanding Magazines*. Ames, Iowa: Iowa State University Press, 1965, $5.95.

RELIGIOUS PRESS

Marty, M. E., *et al*. *Religious Press in America*. New York: Holt, Rinehart and Winston, 1963, $4.00.

TRADE JOURNALS AND HOUSE ORGANS

Baird, Russell N., and Turnbull, Arthur T. *Industrial and Business Journalism*. Philadelphia: Chilton Press, 1961, $5.72.

Elfenbein, Julien. *Business Journalism*. New York: Harper & Row, 1960.

Reddick, Dewitt C., and Crowell, Alfred A. *Industrial Editing*. New York: Matthew Bender & Co., 1962, $7.50.

RADIO AND TELEVISION JOURNALISM

CBS News. *Television News Reporting*. New York: McGraw-Hill, 1958, $5.75.

Deutscher, J. Noel. *Your Future in Television*. New York: Richards Rosen Press, 1963, $2.65.

Lorch, John. *Careers in Broadcasting*. New York: Appleton-Century-Crofts, 1962, $3.95.

PUBLIC RELATIONS

Bernays, Edward L. *Your Future in Public Relations*. New York: Richards Rosen Press, 1961.

Cutlip, Scott M., and Center, A. H. *Effective Public Relations*. Englewood Cliffs, N.J.: Prentice-Hall, 1964, $8.95.

Marston, John E. *Nature of Public Relations*. New York: McGraw-Hill, 1963, $7.95.

FREE-LANCE WRITING

Gabriel, H. W. *How to Write for Money*. Englewood Cliffs, N.J.: Prentice-Hall, 1965, $5.95.

Lobsenz, Norman M. *Writing as a Career*. New York: Henry Z. Walck, 1963, $3.75.

Mathieu, Aron M (ed.) *The Creative Writer*. Cincinnati: *Writer's Digest*, $6.95.

Reynolds, Paul R. *Writing and Selling of Non-Fiction*. New York: Doubleday, 1963, $4.50.

INDEX

Index |